VINTAGE
BOARD GAMES

WHITE STAR PUBLISHERS

VINTAGE BOARD GAMES

HISTORY AND ENTERTAINMENT FROM THE LATE 18TH TO THE BEGINNING OF THE 20TH CENTURY

Text and photos by

Adrian Seville

HET VERMAKELIJK HARLEKIJNSPEL

Het HARLEKIJNSPEL wordt met twee dobbelsteenen gespeeld, waaraan door een onbepaald aantal spelers deelgenomen kan worden. Vooraf bepale men, hoe groot het aantal fiches waarmee men speelt, en legge deze voor zich, waarna ieder een fiche op Nr. 7 zet, een worp met de steenen doe, en hij die het grootste aantal oogen werpt, het spel aanvangt.

Het aantal oogen dat geworpen wordt, is het nummer waarop de speler een fiche zet, is dit nummer echter reeds bezet, dan wint men hetgeen er op staat en

werpt nogmaals tot men een onbezet Nr. getroffen heeft; werpt men echter 7, dan is HARLEKIJN de winner en het voorwerp waarom men speelt gaat in den pot. Men speelt zoolang als men inzet voor zich heeft, heeft men zijn laatste stuk opgezet, dan mag men nog eens op zijne beurt gratis werpen, in de hoop; men een Nr. werpt waar iets opstaat; treft men dat niet dan is men van het spel af. Die het langst zijn inzet heeft wint de POT en bovendien alles wat op de Nummers staat.

J. VLIEGER - AMSTERDAM.

Contents

Game of Harlequin. Amsterdam: Vlieger, about 1890

Introduction

Printed board games first appeared at the end of the sixteenth century, when games such as the Game of the Goose - a simple race game played with dice, as shown in Chapter 1 of this book - spread from Italy to other countries of Europe. At first, these games were simple designs, printed on fragile paper. But the printed board game reached new heights of beauty and ingenuity during the nineteenth century. Indeed, the century began with a golden age for up-market board games, finely engraved and often with glowing hand-color. But these expensive games faced competition from the new process of lithography and by the end of the century mass-produced games from the steam-press were flooding a European-wide market. There were games on almost every conceivable theme, whether on serious subjects like geography or history, or on the crazes of the moment. The games often relied on dice or a small, numbered spinning top called a totum (or teetotum), with no choice of move. Nowadays, the fascination of these games lies not in playing them – though many are still good fun - but in seeing how they reflect the specific cultures of different times and places. Other games were designed for gambling, with a winner scooping the pool. Some, though, were 'mind games', where serious thought was required.

This book presents examples of all these genres and includes games from a wide selection of countries – England, France, Germany, The Netherlands, Belgium, Spain and the USA. It is interesting to see how the focus of the games changed over the century and beyond – for example, how the Game of the Goose, the prototype for so many of the games, was adapted to new markets, so that what had been largely a gambling game for adults became a children's game for family entertainment. Also intended for family use were educational and moral games, designed to shape the development of young people. As transport became easier and more affordable during the century, games which represented a journey took new forms. The stagecoach was replaced by the train or steamboat and, as tourism became more widespread, games which had reflected the aristocrat's Grand Tour were replaced by games such as the Tour of Switzerland, a popular destination. Games reflecting leisure pursuits multiplied and became ever more diverse. However, games with a satirical focus, or a strong political message, were produced throughout the century and were definitely not for children. These games cleverly used pictures to convey their message, as did the many advertising games that began to appear towards the end of the century and grew in variety into the next. Not included in the book are examples of board games such as chess or draughts, where towards the end of the century it became cheaper to produce the boards by printing in color rather than by making them in wood or other materials.

Although the main focus of the book is on European games in all their richness, the final chapter shows how these games shaped the appetite for games in the United States. The games circulating in the USA in the first quarter of the nineteenth century were imported from London and the choice offered in advertisements, whether in New York, Boston or Philadelphia always emphasized the 'new game' of the moment. Even when American games appeared, they were adaptations of familiar European games, though this debt was not always acknowledged. Indeed, one of the most famous American games, the Mansion of Happiness *first published by Ives in 1843, is an unacknowledged adaptation*

of a London game dating from the early 1800s. However, in the second half of the century, American inventiveness came to the fore, most notably in 1860, with Milton Bradley's Checkered Game of Life, *which was to change the impact that board games had on society.*

A striking feature of the games pictured in this book is how sharply they represent the different cultures from which they sprang. Almost every game offers a wealth of detailed images that can be studied from many viewpoints. Costumes, everyday objects, occupations and leisure pastimes all offer rich collections typical of their countries of origin and of their time. But a deeper look at these games will often reveal complex and sometimes disturbing social and cultural attitudes. Readers who would enjoy looking at these games in close-up are invited to browse the Italian web site set up by Dr Luigi Ciompi and the author – www. giochidelloca.it which offers good-quality images of over 2,500 board games, freely downloadable for private use. There is also a full bibliography and a large selection of articles to download, for further study of these fascinating and beautiful games.

8-9 Skating Rink. Paris: Saussine, about 1900

The Game of the Goose and Other Animals

The medieval Game of the Goose – a fast and furious race game popular throughout Europe – was updated in the nineteenth century. Animals often replaced the geese, monkeys caricaturing human behavior lending special humour to the game.

The Game of the Goose *is perhaps the most influential of any printed board game. It has spawned literally thousands of variants over the centuries – all simple dice games played on a spiral track with no choice of move, but on a great variety of themes. Even today, it is still played and new variants continue to be produced, especially in the Netherlands.*

The first records of it come from fifteenth-century Italy, in the form of advice not to play it or indeed as legal prohibitions – a sure sign that the game was popular. This disapproval was because the game was notorious for gambling. Indeed, when the game was sent by Francesco de' Medici to the Court of Philip II of Spain towards the end of the sixteenth century, Philip's jester, known as 'Gonzalillo', wrote complainingly to Francesco: 'Accursed be your servant Luis Dovara, who brought along a devilish game called Gioco dell'Oca *[Game of the Goose], played with two dice.... It is a game played in Tuscany and God grant that he who made it may burn, for the Prince and the Infanta and Luis Tristan*

I have lost 40 scudi.' The game spread through the medium of printing to other countries in Europe at this time and was widely enjoyed for two hundred years. To understand why it was (and still is) such a good game, have a look at the New and entertaining Children's Game of the Goose, for the Youth of the Netherlands. *Although it is presented as 'new', this version of the game, and its rules, would have seemed entirely familiar to Gonzalillo and the Spanish Court. Indeed, this 'classic' version of the game, with only minor rule variations, would have been known across the whole of Western Europe.*

Looking more closely at the game, it is immediately obvious why it gets its name: geese are represented on many of the spaces of the track. Why geese? Probably because geese are considered lucky in Italy – and the geese generally bring luck in the game. If a player's token lands on a goose, the player gets the points from the dice-throw again and immediately moves on, doubling the throw. The game is played with two dice, adding the points together and, on the relatively short track of 63 spaces, this makes for a very lively game. But there is a problem: an initial throw of nine would bring the player to a goose and theoretically the player should then hop forward by another nine points to the goose on space 18, then to the goose on space 27, and so all the way to the winning space. To prevent this, a special rule applies just to the initial throw of nine. This special rule sends the player's token to one of the spaces 26 or 53, marked with a pair of dice showing the particular throw. So, not an immediate win – but still a very lucky throw, especially if you get to space 53, with a chance to win in your very next throw.

But getting to the winning space is normally not so easy. There are several hazards, at each of which the unfortunate player must pay a stake into the winner's pool. The stakes can be small or large – if children play, sweets, nuts or small biscuits are favorites. Most feared of the hazards is death (space 58), where the player must start again. But the well and the prison spaces are also bad: there you must wait for another player to release you, who then takes your place. A welcome feature, which avoids the tedious waiting for an exact throw found in many other race games, is that if you overthrow the winning space your excess points are counted backwards. That can be very exciting. For example, the overthrow may carry you back to the death space, so you must start again. Or it may land you on a goose, where you get your points again – but now the extra points carry you further back. Sometimes the game can go on for many rounds, generating its own excitement. This unpredictability of the classic game helps to account for its success.

We have been looking at how the game is played. But another way of looking at the game is as an allegory of human life. Here the geese represent positive events, perhaps even help from heaven on a spiritual journey towards paradise, while the hazards represent problems along the way. On this interpretation, the first hazard, the bridge at space 6, is a rite of passage into adulthood; the inn at space 19 (where you miss a turn) represents wasting time on earthly pleasures; the well at space 31

grave error for which you need help; the labyrinth at space 42 (where you have to go back) means you have lost your way, the prison at space 52 symbolizes serious fault; and death at space 58 means death of the soul, so that the spiritual journey must start afresh. Interpretations like this are not far-fetched for a medieval game, in an age when symbolism was important. The numerology of the game also supports this analysis: for example, the winning number 63 has been associated from classical times with the 'Grand Climacteric', the major crisis in life supposed to occur at the age of 63 years. And the positioning of the geese, in a double series each spaced by nine, recalls the mystic religious significance of that number as the 'Trinity of Trinities'. But by the nineteenth century, such ideas were long forgotten and the Game of the Goose was just a game to be played.

Het vernieuwd vermakelijk Kinder Ganze Spel, voor de Ned

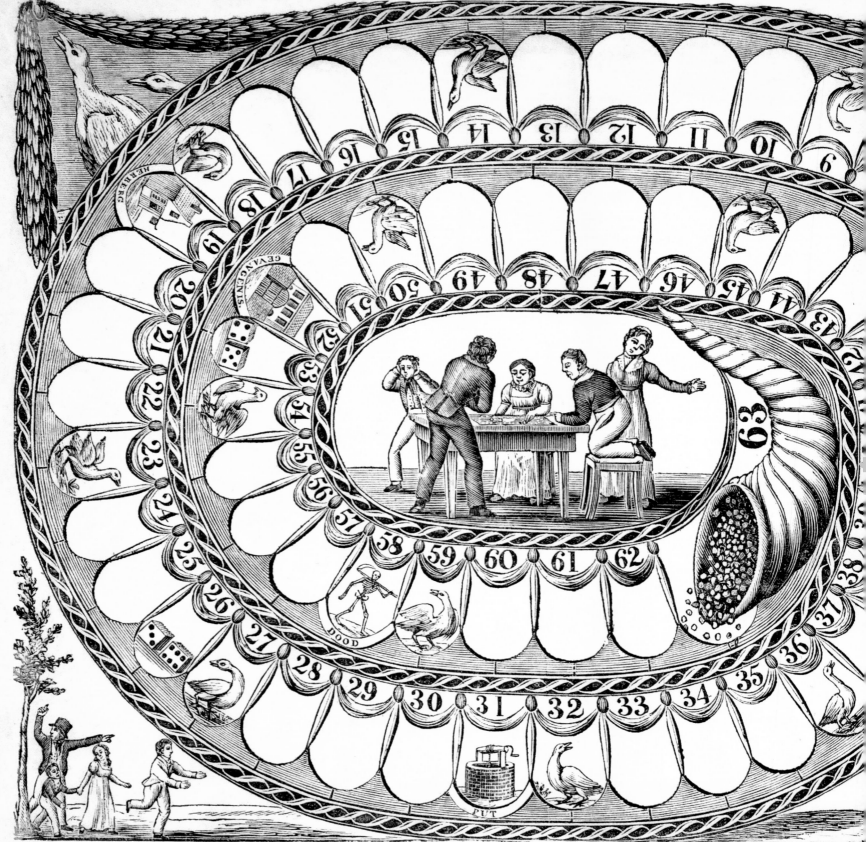

REGLEMENT OP HET VERNIEUWD VERMAKELIJK KINDER GANZE SPE

I. Men neemt twee dobbelsteenen, welke aan alle zijde met oogen geteekend zijn.

II. Men werpt met de steenen, wie eerst speelt.

III. Die in het begin, of de eerste reis, 6 en 3 oogen werpt gaat tot No. 26, en die 5 en 4 oogen werpt, zet zich op No. 53.

IV. Die werpt, dat hij op een GANS komt, mag nog weder voorstellen, zoo veel oogen, als hij heeft geworpen, tot dat hij komt, daar waar *geen* GANS staat.

V. Die werpt dat hij op de BRUG komt, betaald, doch die dubbeld betalen wil, gaat tot No. 12.

VI. Die werpt, dat hij in de HERBERG komt, moet zijn gelag betalen, en zijn beurt éens laten voorbij gaan.

VII. Die werpt, dat hij in de PUT komt, moet betalen, en zoo lang blijven staan, tot dat hij van een ander verlost word.

VIII. Die werpt dat hij in den DOOLHOF komt, moet betalen en drie oogen weder terug tellen.

IX. Die werpt, dat hij in de GEVANGENIS komt, moet sluitgeld betalen, en zoo lang blijven, tot dat hij weder van een ander verlost word.

X. Die werpt dat hij op de DOOD komt, moet betalen en weder op nieuw, van voren af beginnen te spelen.

Te Zalt-Bommel, bij JOHANNES NOMAN, Boekdrukker.

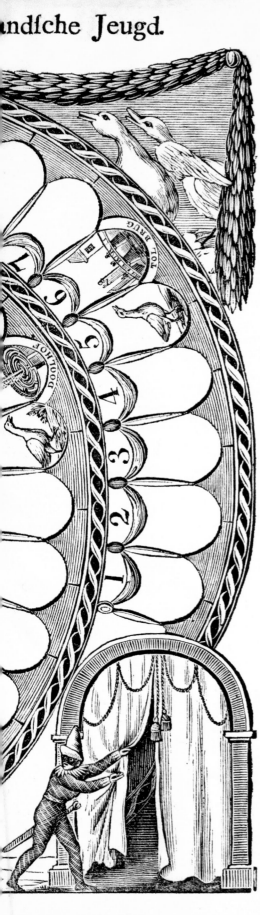

Die van een ander achterhaald, en op
.. le nommer komt, betaald en gaat op
..lfde nommer terug.
.. Die werpt, dat hij op over 63 komt,
..ld zijn overig getal zoo veel terug, en
..t op een GANS valt, moet hij nog zoo
..rug tellen.
.. Die in 63 werpt, wint de geheele pot,
..elt weder eerst.

*New and entertaining Children's Game
of the Goose, for the Youth
of the Netherlands. Zalt-Bommel: Noman
about 1825*

However good a game it was, by the beginning of the nineteenth century the Game of the Goose was regarded as old fashioned, at least by adults, and a gradual shift towards its becoming a game for children began. One of the earliest markers of this shift is this game from the Netherlands, which has a central decoration showing the game being played by young people. It is obviously creating much excitement – the boy on the left can hardly bear to watch. The game is nicely engraved, with a fine image of Death on space 58, striding forward with his scythe on his shoulder. Later versions of the game for children often toned down the death space, using a less disturbing image. The winning space at the end shows a large 'horn of plenty' instead of the garden of paradise often shown there.

Game of the Goose.
Épinal: Pinot & Sagaire
about 1860

Although the next game, a French example dating from about 1860, looks very different from the Netherlands game, it is still the same classic Game of the Goose (Jeu de l'oie in French). The main difference is that the non-active spaces, where the player's token simply rests on landing, are no longer blank but are decorated with lively images. These are intended to make the game more attractive but have the disadvantage that they compete visually with the active spaces (the geese and the hazards) and so make the game less easy to play. In this example, the scenes decorating the track do not have a linking theme but are just for children to enjoy. In the lower left corner, a young man is shown playing the game against a girl: 'You lose, mademoiselle – I have 63!' This game was produced at Épinal, in a provincial region in the North-East of France, where mass production of printed images – not just games but all sorts of popular prints - grew into a major international industry. The game is inexpensively produced, on cheap machine-made paper, and the coloring is crudely done, using a different stencil for each color dabbed on with a *pochoir*, a little cloth pad. The playing tokens are printed at the side, to be cut out and stuck together.

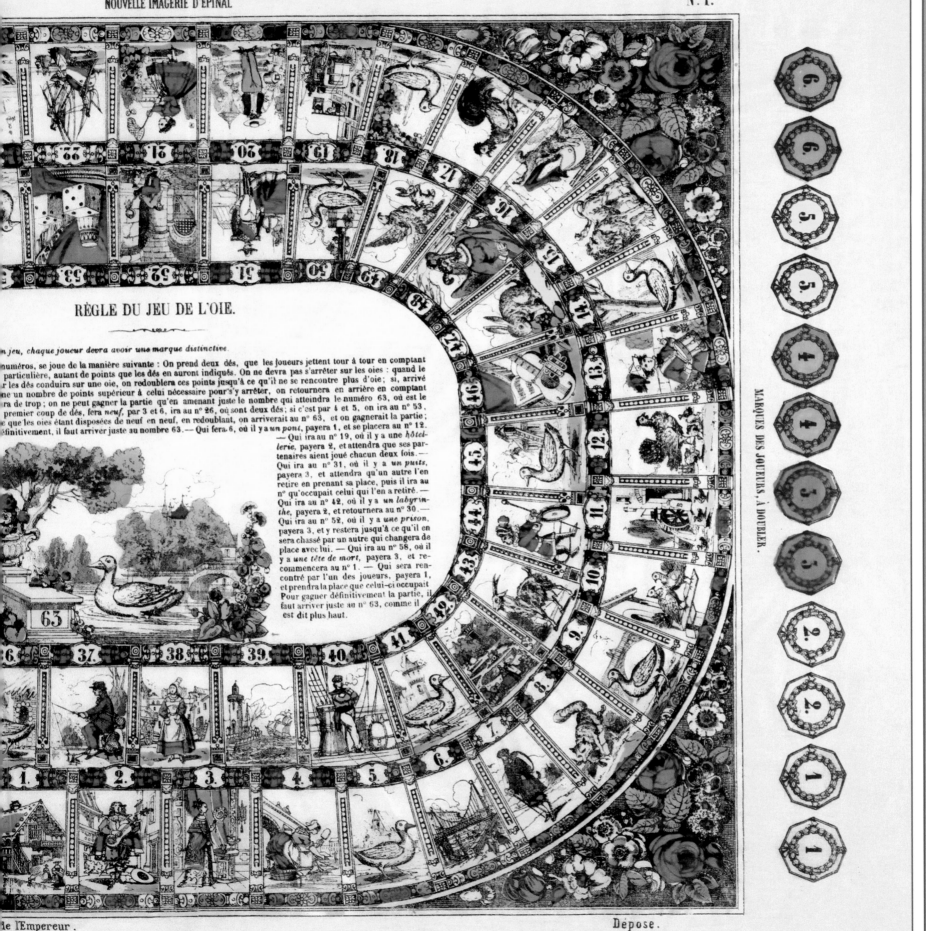

RÈGLE DU JEU DE L'OIE.

…n jeu, chaque joueur devra avoir *une marque distinctive.*

…numéros, se joue de la manière suivante : On prend deux dés, que les joueurs jettent tour à tour en comptant …particulière, autant de points que les dés en auront indiqués. On ne devra pas s'arrêter sur les oies : quand le …r les dés conduira sur une oie, on redoublera ces points jusqu'à ce qu'il ne se rencontre plus d'oie ; si, arrivé …ne un nombre de points supérieur à celui nécessaire pour s'y arrêter, on retournera en arrière en comptant …ra de trop ; on ne peut gagner la partie qu'en amenant juste le nombre qui atteindra le numéro 63, où est le …premier coup de dés, fera *neuf*, par 3 et 6, ira au n° 26, où sont deux dés ; si c'est par 4 et 5, on ira au n° 53, …e que les oies étant disposées de neuf en neuf, en redoublant, on arrivera au n° 63, et on gagnerait la partie ; …définitivement, il faut arriver juste au nombre 63. — Qui fera 6, où il y a *un pont*, payera 1, et se placera au n° 12.

— Qui ira au n° 19, où il y a une *hôtellerie*, payera 2, et attendra que ses partenaires aient joué chacun deux fois. — Qui ira au n° 31, où il y a *un puits*, payera 3, et attendra qu'un autre l'en retire en prenant sa place, puis il ira au n° qu'occupait celui qui l'en a retiré. — Qui ira au n° 42, où il y a *un labyrinthe*, payera 2, et retournera au n° 30. — Qui ira au n° 52, où il y a *une prison*, payera 3, et y restera jusqu'à ce qu'il en sera chassé par un autre qui changera de place avec lui. — Qui ira au n° 58, où il y a *une tête de mort*, payera 3, et recommencera au n° 1. — Qui sera rencontré par l'un des joueurs, payera 1, et prendra la place que celui-ci occupait. Pour gagner définitivement la partie, il faut arriver juste au n° 63, comme il est dit plus haut.

MARQUES DES JOUEURS, À DOUBLER.

…le l'Empereur.   Déposé.

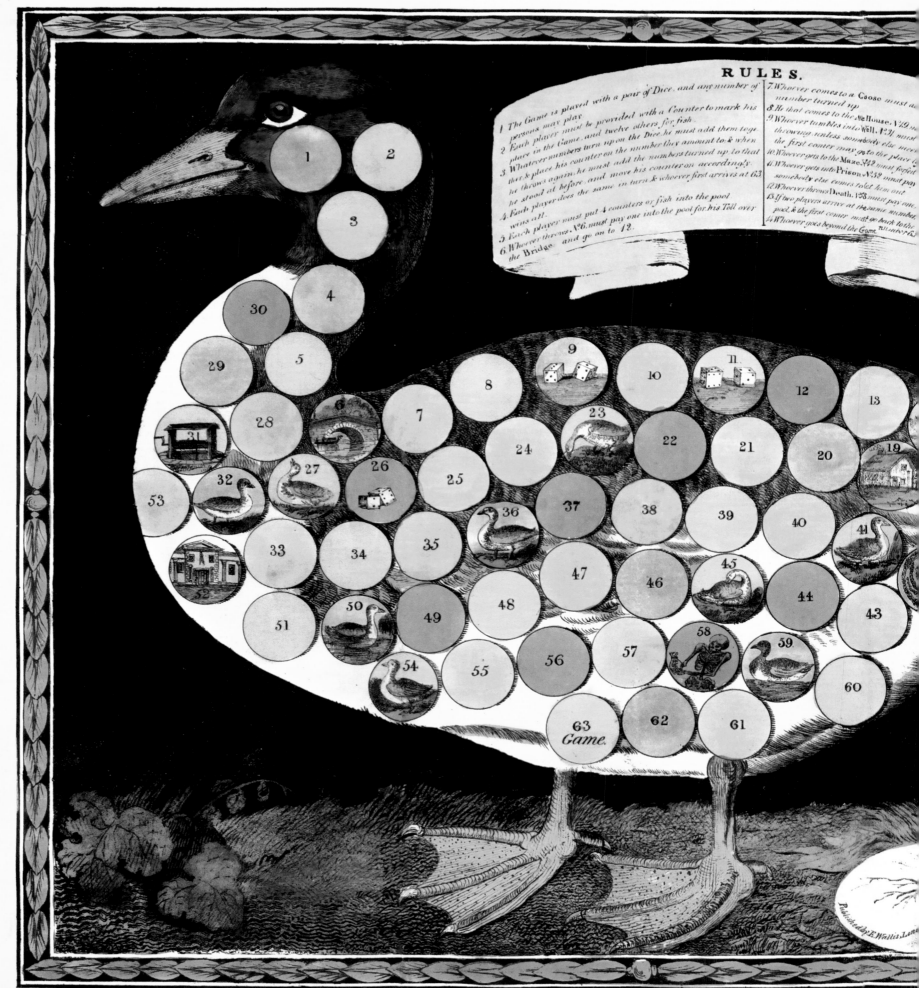

THE ROYAL GAME of GOO

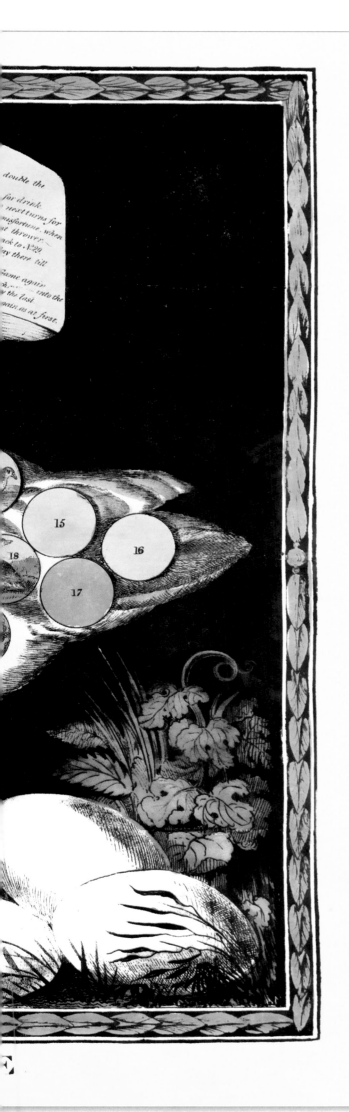

The Royal Game of Goose.

London: Edward Wallis

about 1840

Games in the form of a goose were first produced at the beginning of the century. This example, by Edward Wallis of London (as indicated in tiny writing on one of the eggs), dates from about 1840, when the popularity of the Game of the Goose in England was diminishing. The impact of the large goose image is quite striking but the game is almost unaltered from the classic version. The main difference is that the first two geese are missing from the track, as was often the case in English Goose games. This means that there is no need for a special rule for the initial throw of nine and so no chance of a quick win. Maybe the puritanical English thought it would be unfair to win too quickly, so that they abolished these geese. The rules say that each player must have twelve counters 'for fish' – this is a corruption of the French word *fiches*, meaning counters used as stakes in the game. English counters were often shaped like fish, following the pun.

Game of the Goose.
Milan: Eliseo Macchi

about 1900

Some Games of the Goose have an extension of the classic game from 63 to 90 spaces. This comes from Italy, where the number 90 is regarded as particularly lucky, since it is the number of balls from which the Italian State Lottery is drawn. One of the first fruits of Italian unification after the 1860s was that the various provincial lotteries were brought together, creating huge interest in gambling. The producers of the game, anxious to hedge their bets, say that by prior agreement it can be played in the old way, ending at space 63. There was no difficulty in extending the series of geese, spaced by nine, to the end of the track, but new hazards had to be invented: the *fountain* at space 71, which acts as a block, and the *tower* at space 82, where the rule is as for the *prison*.

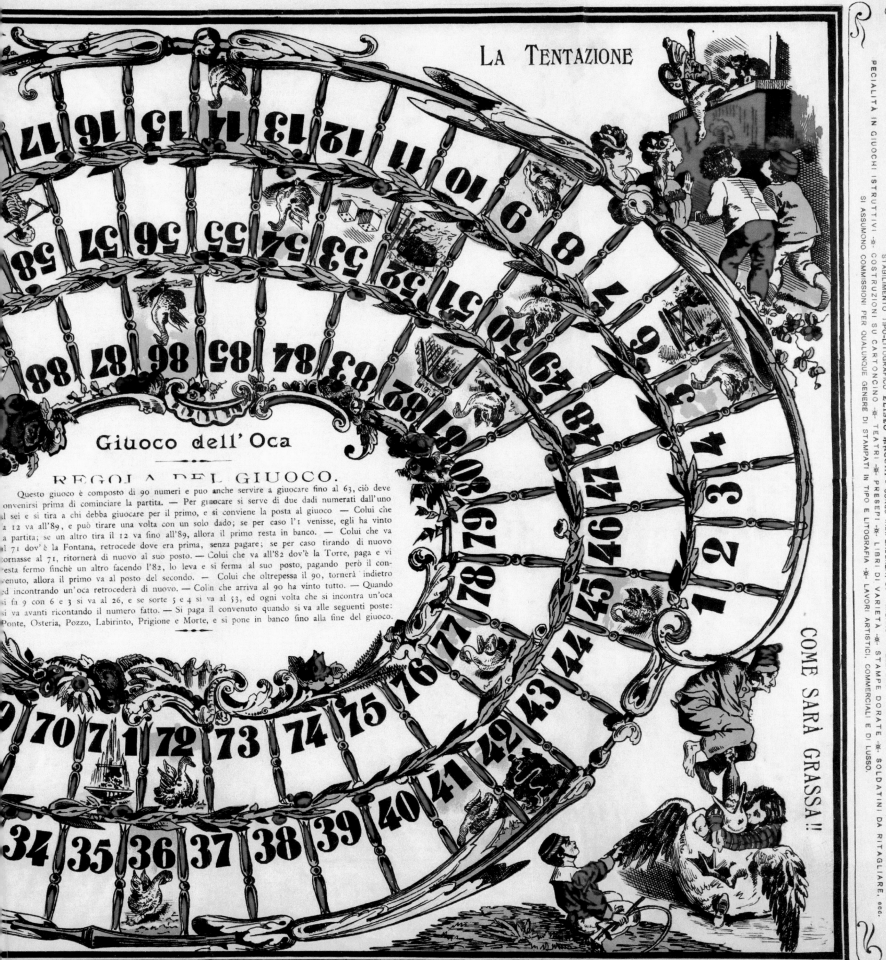

La Tentazione

Giuoco dell'Oca

REGOLA DEL GIUOCO.

Questo giuoco è composto di 90 numeri e può anche servire a giuocare fino al 63, ciò deve convenirsi prima di cominciare la partita. — Per giuocare si serve di due dadi numerati dall'uno al sei e si tira a chi debba giuocare per il primo, e si conviene la posta al giuoco — Colui che va 12 va all'89, e può tirare una volta con un solo dado; se per caso l'1 venisse, egli ha vinto la partita; se un altro tira il 12 va fino all'89, allora il primo resta in banco. — Colui che va al 71 dov'è la Fontana, retrocede dove era prima, senza pagare; se per caso tirando di nuovo tornasse al 71, ritornerà di nuovo al suo posto. — Colui che va all'82 dov'è la Torre, paga e vi resta fermo finchè un altro facendo l'82, lo leva e si ferma al suo posto, pagando però il convenuto, allora il primo va al posto del secondo. — Colui che oltrepassa il 90, tornerà indietro ed incontrando un'oca retrocederà di nuovo. — Colin che arriva al 90 ha vinto tutto. — Quando si fa 9 con 6 e 3 si va al 26, e se sorte 5 e 4 si va al 53, ed ogni volta che si incontra un'oca si va avanti ricontando il numero fatto. — Si paga il convenuto quando si va alle seguenti poste: Ponte, Osteria, Pozzo, Labirinto, Prigione e Morte, e si pone in banco fino alla fine del giuoco.

COME SARÀ GRASSA!!

STABILIMENTO TIPO-LITOGRAFICO ELISEO MACCHI - CORSO INDIPENDENZA, 24 - MILANO - TELEFONO: 11-96. SPECIALITÀ IN GIUOCHI ISTRUTTIVI ✳ COSTRUZIONI SU CARTONCINO ✳ TEATRI ✳ PRESEPI ✳ LIBRI DI VARIETÀ ✳ STAMPE DORATE ✳ SOLDATINI DA RITAGLIARE, ecc. SI ASSUMONO COMMISSIONI PER QUALUNQUE GENERE DI STAMPATI IN TIPO E LITOGRAFIA ✳ LAVORI ARTISTICI, COMMERCIALI E DI LUSSO.

Stab. Lit.-Tip. E. Macchi - Milano.

New Improved Goose Game. Nuremberg: Campe

about 1820

German Games of the Goose in the nineteenth century were anything but classic, showing great variation in their rules. The *New Improved Goose Game*, although it has the classic 63 spaces, has several different features, including variant images for some of the classic hazards. The most interesting feature is that the geese (just a single series rather than the usual double series) are depicted facing either forwards or backwards along the track. As the printed rules make clear, those facing forward act as normal throw-doubling spaces; but those facing the other way act as stops, so that the player must not advance. This rule seems to be found explicitly only in German games; but in the Netherlands a similar rule can be played by agreement among the players, though not written down.

Neues verbessertes Gänse-Spiel.

No 844.   Nürnberg bei Fr. Nap. Campe.

(Regeln.) Dieses Spiel wird mit zwei Würfeln gespielt. Jeder Spieler sext 12 Marken in die Casse No 63. Wer mit dem ersten Wurf 5 und 4 wirft, geht sogleich auf No 53, worauf er ein beliebiges Zeichen sext, wirft er 6 und 3. so kömt er auf No 26. Wer 6 wirft, zahlt 3 Marken in die Casse und kömt auf No 12. Wer auf No 19 kömt, muß so lange aussetzen, bis die übrigen Spieler zweimal geworfen haben. Wer auf No 31 kömt, sext so lange aus, bis einer der Mitspieler gleiche Numer trifft und nimt dan deßen früheren Platz ein. Wer auf No 42 kömt, zahlt 3 Marken und geht auf No 30 zurück. Wer auf No 52 kömt, zahlt 3 Marken und bleibt so lange bis ein anderer ihn ablöst, deßen Platz er dann einnimt. Wer auf No 58 kömt, zahlt 3 Marken und muß das Spiel von Vornen beginnen. Wer auf eine rückwärts gehende Gans zu stehen kömt, zahlt 3 Marken u. geht um das doppelte seines Wurfes zurück, wer hingegen auf eine vorwärts stehende Gans kömt, deßen Wurf zahlt doppelt und geht er um so viel weiter. Wer endlich auf No 63 kömt, hat das Spiel, mit dem darin befindlichen Einsatze gewonnen.

Game of the Monkeys. Metz: Delhalt

about 1880

A popular way of updating the Goose game was to substitute monkeys for the geese. This was not a new idea: in fact a game with just this substitution was printed in Italy as far back as 1588, so of an age comparable to the earliest printed Games of the Goose. The enthusiasm in art for showing monkeys as caricatures of human figures (*singerie*) has been strong in different periods but the nineteenth century produced many examples, and printed games followed the trend. Sometimes the monkey games were exact substitutions within a classic Game of the Goose as in the *Game of the Monkeys*, produced in Metz in the North-East of France. Here the main interest is in the witty caricatures of monkeys along the track, all shown doing very human things, like smoking, going for a well-dressed promenade or unsuccessfully trying to catch a butterfly; but the decorations outside the track are also worth a look, particularly the two monkeys at the lower edge who are competing strenuously at dice.

Ce jeu se joue avec deux Dés, les joueurs mettent leur enjeu. Le premier qui arrive au N.º 63 gagne la partie. Le premier joueur jette les dés et amène un nombre de points qui lui indiquent la place où il doit mettre sa marque, et ainsi de suite pour tous les joueurs. Si l'on amène 6 et 3 ce qui fait 9 il se place au N.º 26, s'il amène 5 et 4 il va à 53 qui est le Labyrinthe et y reste jusqu'à ce qu'un autre joueur le déplace. Si un joueur fait 6 qui est le Pont il paye l'amande qui est la valeur de la mise. S'il arrive au N.º 19 qui est le Cabaret, il paye l'amande et reste deux tours sans jouer afin d'avoir le temps de se rafraichir. S'il arrive au N.º 32 qui est le Puits il paye l'amande et y reste jusqu'à ce qu'un joueur vienne le retirer. S'il arrive au N.º 31 qui est le fort, il payera l'amande double et restera 4 tours sans jouer pour qu'il ait le temps de le visiter. S'il arrive au N.º 53 qui est le Labyrinthe il payera l'amande et reste un tour sans jouer. S'il arrive à la mort il payera l'amande double pour faire son enterrement et recommanca à jouer. enfin s'il arrive au N.º 63 il gagne toutes les mises et les amandes mais s'il amène plus de points qu'il ne lui en faut pour arriver juste au N.º gagnant, il recule d'autant de points qu'il en a de trop.   DÉPOSÉ.

Fabrique d'Estampes de   DELHALT. Metz.

The New Game of the Monkey. London: Wallis

1820

Our second monkey game is English. *The New Game of the Monkey* looks at first to be a standard 63-space Goose game with monkeys instead of geese, but in fact has several differences. Instead of the usual doubling of the throw, there are individual rules for monkey spaces. For example, the *Dancing Monkeys* must pay one stake for learning to Dance, the *Soldier* may march to No. 13, and the *Dandy* must pay two stakes for his folly. However, the hazard spaces are very like those in Goose, and are placed identically. For example, at the *Bridge you* must pay one stake for Toll, at the *Inn* you must stop a turn and drink, at the *Well* you must stop till someone comes and helps you out, while space 58, showing the suicidal *Gamester*, is just like the death space, so that you must begin again.

The corner decorations are entertaining, though they have nothing to do with playing the game. One shows a judge bemused by a red herring, while on the floor is a book entitled 'Black …' (Blackstone's *Commentaries on the Laws of England*). The opposite corner shows two monkeys whipping a dog tied by a cord to a saucepan. Above, a monkey admires itself in a looking-glass, while in the final corner a monkey is caught in a steel trap — possibly an anti-slavery image? The 'lady' courted at space 14 wears a saucepan as a hat, rather like Tenniel's illustration of Tweedledum in Lewis Carroll's much later *Through the Looking-Glass*.

The monkey at space 23 is dressed as Little Red Riding Hood, while the one at space 18 wears a bellows as a hat. A rather wonderful English madness!

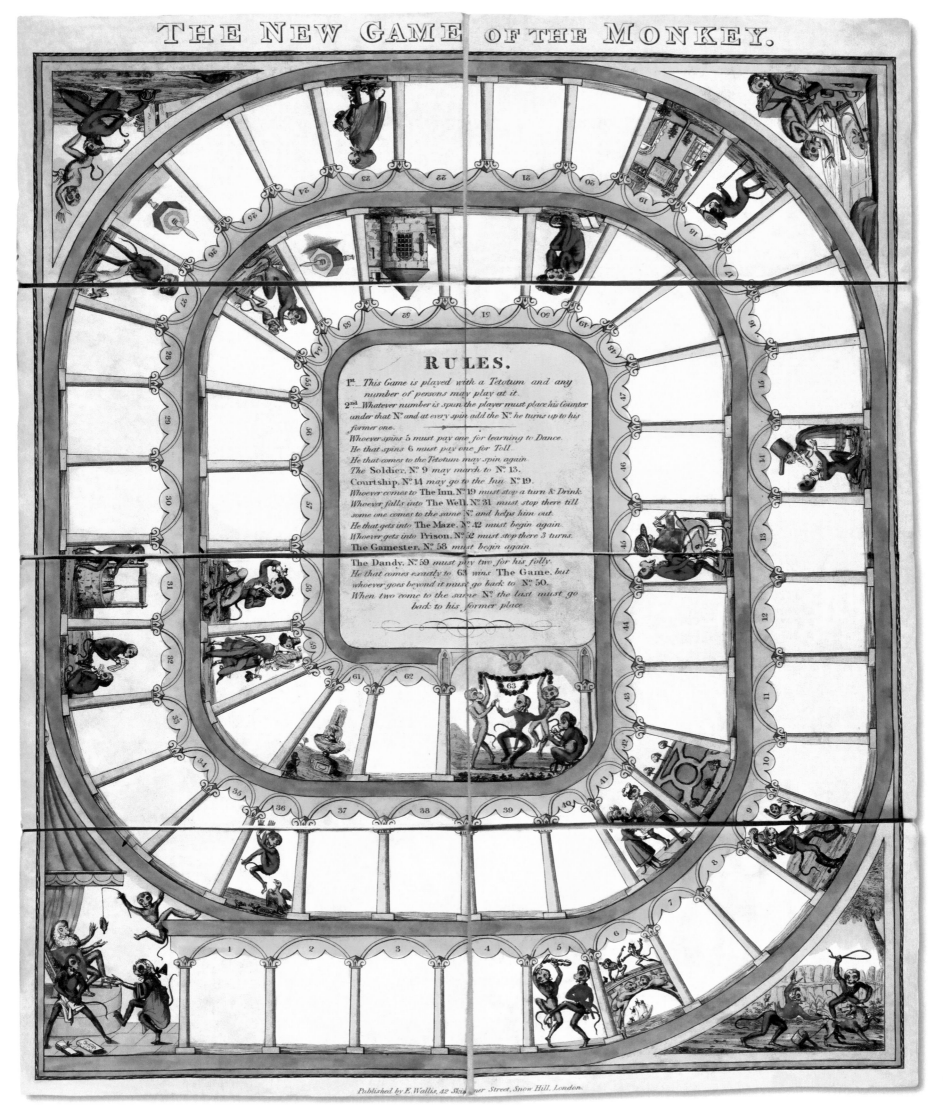

THE NEW GAME OF THE MONKEY.

RULES.

1st__ This Game is played with a Tetotum and any number of persons may play at it.

2nd__ Whatever number is spun the player must place his Counter under that No. and at every spin add the No. he turns up to his former one.

Whoever spins 5 must pay one for learning to Dance.

He that spins 6 must pay one for Toll.

He that comes to the Tetotum may spin again.

The Soldier, No. 9 may march to No. 13.

Courtship, No. 14 may go to the Inn. No. 19.

Whoever comes to The Inn, No. 19 must stop a turn & Drink.

Whoever falls into The Well, No. 31 must stop there till some one comes to the same No. and helps him out.

He that gets into The Maze, No. 42 must begin again.

Whoever gets into Prison, No. 52 must stop there 3 turns.

The Gamester, No. 58 must begin again.

The Dandy, No. 59 must pay two for his folly.

He that comes exactly to 63 wins The Game, but whoever goes beyond it must go back to No. 50.

When two come to the same No. the last must go back to his former place.

Published by E. Wallis, 42 Skinner Street, Snow Hill, London.

London: Published by William Spooner 379 Strand Nov.r 5th 1849

26

The Hare and the Tortoise.

London: Spooner

1859

Other animals were pressed into service in updating the Game of the Goose. *The Hare and the Tortoise*, published in London in 1859 as a beautiful color lithograph, breaks new ground by dividing the track of the game between a splendid picture of the tortoise and an even more splendid picture of the hare. The track starts at the hare's rear left foot, winds about between its back legs until space 8 is reached — but space 9 is found on the tortoise — after which the track switches back to the hare before heading off again. Some of the spaces depict a small image of a hare, where the player must miss a turn and pay two counters to the pool. Others, showing a tortoise, act as throw-doubling spaces, as in the Game of the Goose, while many of the spaces on the tortoise itself reward the player with three counters. Finally, there are hazard spaces, reminiscent of the Game of the Goose, with which this game shares the characteristic track length of 63 spaces. The player needs to be alert in finding where to move: any player 'who carries his mark to a wrong number must pay 2 to the pool'.

New Game of the Hare.

Weissenberg: G Burkhardt's successors

late 19th century

Hunting has always been a favorite pastime of the German people and the *New Game of the Hare* brings this to the game board. It is a simple game, played with two dice, but the rules are not obvious from the pictures. For example, spaces 34, 45, 58 and 64, all of which have a picture of a hare, act as stops, sending you back to the space from which you made the throw. Other spaces with a picture of a hare have no such effect. In the author's example of the game, a previous owner has marked the unfavorable spaces with a cross, to help in remembering the rules. For example, space 57, showing a bewildered hunter who has presumably lost sight of the hare, requires the player to start again.

Dieses Spiel wird mit zwei Würfeln gespielt und jeder Spieler versieht sich mit einem anderen Zeichen, um die geworfene Nummer zu besetzen. Jeder Spieler setzt 6 Marken in die Kasse. Wer beim Anspielen 1 und 6 wirft, erhält 3 Marken aus der Kasse und geht auf Nr. 12. Wirft man beim Anspielen 1 und 2, so setzt man sein Zeichen auf Nr. 26. Wirft man beim Anspielen 12, so zahlt man 6 Marken in die Kasse. Auf Nr. 19 zahlt man 4 Marken in die Kasse. Wer auf die Hasen 34, 45, 58 und 64 kommt, zahlt 2 Marken und geht auf seinen letzten Platz zurück. Auf Nr. 57 bezahlt der Spieler 3 Marken in die Kasse und fängt von vorne an zu spielen. Auf Nr. 60 muß man sitzen bleiben bis jeder Spieler 3 Mal gewürfelt hat. Wer auf Nr. 67 kommt, darf nicht mehr mitspielen. Würfe über Nr. 73 hinaus werden zurückgezählt. Wer auf Nr. 73 kommt, hat das Spiel gewonnen.

Druck und Verlag von C. Burckardt's Nachfolger in Weißenburg (Elsaß).

Deponirt.

The Game of the Owl: and Other Lotteries

In the Game of the Owl, players paid stakes into a pool, or took from it according to the dice – throw sixes and you scoop the pool. Simple gambling games like this appeared on many themes.

This chapter is concerned with 'lottery' games of various kinds. Some are 'pool' games, played with dice for stakes which are paid into or taken from a pot, which eventually goes to the winner. One of the oldest forms is the Game of the Owl. *This is completely different from the race games of the previous chapter, though it has often been wrongly described as a variation on the* Game of the Goose. *In fact, it is questionable whether it should be considered as a board game at all. Although there is a game sheet, there are no playing pieces and the sheet is really just a set of instructions as to when to pay to the winner's pool of stakes and when to take from it. There are versions which use two dice and versions which use three, but all versions show every possible combination of the dice used, so that each throw gives rise to a clear instruction as to how many stakes to put in the 'pot' or how many to take out. In many*

forms of the game, the end comes when a player throws all sixes – and thereby takes all that is in the pot. However, some forms of the game are more demanding. In these, each player continues until he (it is usually a 'he'!) runs out of money. When all but one have dropped out, the remaining player ('the last man standing') takes what is in the pot. As in the Game of the Goose, *the playing principles of the* Game of the Owl *were easily adapted to new themes.*

The oldest known version of the game survives in a unique print made in the Montorgueil district of Paris early in the seventeenth century, now in the Bibliothèque nationale de France. However, the game is probably even older: its name derives from the German folk stories of Till Eulenspiegel, known in print from the early sixteenth century but perhaps a century earlier in origin. Till is a native of Brunswick who roams across Europe playing practical jokes on all and sundry, exposing their vices as he does so, and the game sheets often picture some of his juicier exploits.

Another kind of lottery game was the German Game of

Seven, *known from about 1600. It was always played with double dice. Here the game board acts as a staking layout, with spaces numbered from two to twelve, space seven being in the center, the others being usually in a circle around it. The rules are simple. You add the numbers on the two dice to get your throw. For any throw except two (i.e. double one) or twelve (double six) or seven, you place a coin on the game sheet at the number thrown, provided that point is empty. If it is not, you take the coin on that point. If you throw seven, you add a coin to the space in the center, where the stakes can build up without limit. If you throw two, you take all the money on the numbers in the circle surrounding the center. If you throw twelve, you take all the money on the game sheet, including the money on the seven space. This game, too, is adaptable to many themes. The most notorious variant, because of its anti-Semitic connotations, is the* Game of the Jew, *where a caricatured figure of a Jew is shown counting up his money in the central space.*

Both the Game of the Owl *and the* Game of Seven *were* out-and-out gambling games, in their original forms most definitely associated with the low-life of the tavern. But in the nineteenth century, variations of them as nicely-printed games with innocuous images were welcomed into the *salon for amusement of the middle and upper classes.*

A third kind of lottery game is modeled on the Giuoco Romano *[Roman Game] or* Biribissi, *known in Italy as early as the sixteenth century. In this, small pictures on card are drawn out of a bag or hat by each player in turn. A game board, bearing the same images, serves as a staking layout. A banker collects the stakes and pays out at fixed odds. Often, a printed sheet of thick card is used, with a double set of matching images. One set is to be cut out and mixed in the bag, while the other set remains intact and forms the staking layout. A variant of this is a sheet with a single set of images to be cut out and drawn from the bag. In this version, each image bears an instruction as to how much to pay into or take from the pool, much as in the* Game of the Owl. *In the nineteenth century, this made a popular and attractive game for children.*

Game of the Owl. Turnhout: Brepols

about 1845

This Belgian example of the *Game of the Owl* is played with three dice and every possible combination of points that can be thrown on the dice is illustrated on the board, each with its own instruction. If there is a 'B' (from the Flemish *betaal*, meaning 'pay') then the specified number of stakes must be paid to the pool. Similarly, if there is a 'T' (from the Flemish *trek*, meaning 'draw') the specified number of stakes must be taken from the pool. The best throws are when the same number appears on all three dice. These throws take half the pool, except that the throw of three sixes takes all of it and the game starts afresh.

That this game celebrates the stories of Eulenspiegel [German for 'owl-glass', with 'glass' as in looking-glass] is confirmed by the central illustration of an owl next to a mirror. However, this version has been sanitized for the nineteenth-century market, so that the images are innocuous. Some, though, are quite witty: the throw of 6,6,1 leads to a picture of soap bubbles, with the instruction *niet* - [do nothing, neither pay nor take].

Uitlegging.

Ten 1. Zal men bespreken wat ieder zal inleggen om te beginnen en dan werpen wie eerst spelen zal; die de hoogste oogen werpt, speelt eerst, en voorts met de zon om.

» 2. Geworpen hebbende, zoekt uw getal, en is 't eene B, zoo betaalt, en is 't eene T, zoo trekt volgens de getallen.

» 3. Wie drie gelijken werpt trekt den halven Pot, doch de oneffen penning blijft bij 't spel.

» 4. Wie drie zessen werpt, trekt den geheelen Pot, en dan moet elk wederom inzetten om te beginnen.

» 5. Die werpt daar NIET staat, zal voor dien tijd niets trekken.

Explication.

1. On conviendra d'abord de l'enjeu, puis on jettera les dés pour savoir qui jouera le premier : ce sera celui qui amènera le plus de points et ainsi de suite selon le cours du soleil.

2. Les dés jetés, on cherche son point. Si c'est un B, on paie, si, au contraire, c'est un T on retire du jeu une somme égale à celle que le chiffre indique.

3. Quiconque amènera trois points égaux, gagnera la moitié de la poule, mais le denier impair reste acquis au jeu.

4. Quiconque amènera les trois six, gagne la poule entière, et tous les joueurs doivent faire une nouvelle mise avant de pouvoir recommencer.

5. Quiconque tombera sur le point où se trouve le mot NIET, ne touche rien de cette fois.

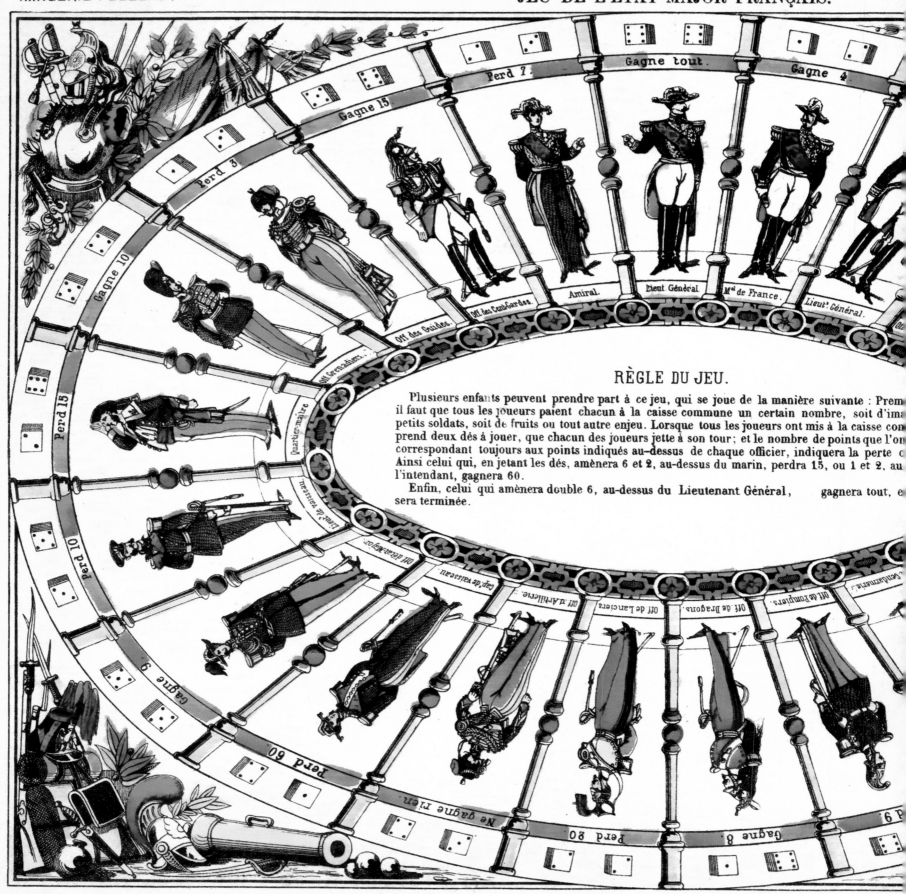

Gagne tout.

Perd 7.

Gagne 4

Gagne 15

Perd 3

Gagne 10

Perd 15

Perd 10

Gagne 9

Perd 60

Ne gagne rien.

Perd 20

Gagne 8

Off. des Guides.

Off. des Cent-Gardes.

Amiral.

Lieut Général.

M.al de France.

Lieut. Général.

Off. Grenadiers...

Quartier-maitre

Lieut. de vaisseau

Off. d'état-major

Cap.ne de vaisseau.

Off. d'Artillerie.

Off. de Lanciers.

Off. de Dragons.

Off. de Tompliers.

RÈGLE DU JEU.

Plusieurs enfants peuvent prendre part à ce jeu, qui se joue de la manière suivante : Prem
il faut que tous les joueurs paient chacun à la caisse commune un certain nombre, soit d'ima
petits soldats, soit de fruits ou tout autre enjeu. Lorsque tous les joueurs ont mis à la caisse com
prend deux dés à jouer, que chacun des joueurs jette à son tour; et le nombre de points que l'on
correspondant toujours aux points indiqués au-dessus de chaque officier, indiquera la perte o
Ainsi celui qui, en jetant les dés, amènera 6 et 2, au-dessus du marin, perdra 15, ou 1 et 2, au
l'intendant, gagnera 60.

Enfin, celui qui amènera double 6, au-dessus du Lieutenant Général, gagnera tout, e
sera terminée.

Game of the French General Military Staff.
Épinal: Pellerin

about 1880

$\mathbf{T}$he *Game of the French Miltary Staff* is a French adaptation of the *Game of the Owl*, where the théme presents officers of the French armed forces. The game is played with two dice, each possible outcome being associated with a particular officer. The winning throw of double six is associated with the Lieutenant-General – in an earlier edition, Napoleon III was identified with this throw. It may seem surprising that The Marshal of France is not associated with the winning throw but in the 19th century that was merely an honorific appointment, rather than being the title of the leader of the French armed forces. The text explains that the game is intended for children and is to be played for: 'images, toy soldiers, fruit or other stakes' – conclusive evidence that what was once a tavern game had been adapted for polite society. This game was produced by the famous firm of Pellerin in Épinal, known for the *Images d'Épinal*. Their cheap stencil-colored woodcuts of military subjects, characters from stories, religious prints, and toys to make from card (among many other themes) were widely distributed throughout the 19th century, not just in France. The company still exists today.

Game of the Ship. Milan: Tamburini

about 1860

The Italian *Gioco della Barca* (Game of the Ship) is a version of the *Game of Seven*, played, like that game, with two dice. The rules, given in Italian on the game sheet, are exactly those for the *Game of Seven* outlined in the introduction to this chapter, so that the stakes build up on the ship in the center when anyone throws seven. This Milanese example comes from the earlier years of the nineteenth century and shows fairly careful hand coloring by brush, rather than the stencil coloring of later mass production. The bold image of the ship, bristling with cannon, is a woodcut but the rules are printed from type, within a decorative stereotype border. This was a reasonably economical way of producing an attractive print of medium quality, as compared with the expensive engraving of a copper plate, as favored by the up-market printing houses.

IL VERO GIUOCO DELLA BARCA

DICHIARAZIONE SOPRA IL GIUOCO DELLA BARCA.

Al Giuoco della Barca si pigliano due dadi disegnati da tutte le parti: poi si fa chi prima debba tirare, quindi s'incomincia.

I. Chi fa 3. 4. 5. 6. 8. 9. 10. 11. metterà sopra i detti numeri una moneta, e se nei suddetti numeri vi è qualche moneta si leva.

II. Chi fa 7. metterà sempre una moneta in Barca.

III. Chi fa 2. leverà tutte le monete che si trovano sopra i numeri all'intorno.

IV. Chi fa 12. leverà tutte le monete che si trovano sopra i numeri ed anche quelli che si trovano nella Barca.

Si vende in Milano nella Stamperia di Gio. Tamburini in contrada di S. Raffaele.

Onderrichting hoe men dit spel moet spelen. Dit spel kan onder zoo veel personen gespeeld worden als men begeert. Men bedingt vooraf, hoeveel geld ieder speler voor zich nemen zal, terwijl zij allen even veel moeten hebben ; bij voorbeeld : ieder 10 cents of halve cents, naar verkiezing. Men neemt een paar dobbelsteenen aan alle kanten geteekend, en werpt wie beginnen zal. Zoo veel oogen iemand werpt, moet hij op hetzelfde nummer een zijner geldstukken zetten : zoo dit nummer reeds met een geldstuk bezet is, dan neemt hij het er af, b. v. zoo hij 6 oogen werpt, en die 6 met een cent bezet is, dan neemt hij die cent als winst, en werpt ten tweeden male, tot dat hij een onbezet nummer werpt, hetwelk hij dan met een geldstuk moet bezetten. Indien men 7 werpt, dan is de Arlequin de winnaar van het in te zetten geldstuk, en alles blijft in den zak, zonder dat iemand er iets uit lichten moge. Zoo lang iemand der spelers van zijne geldstukken heeft, werpt hij op zijne beurt: als het geld op is, kan hij nog eens vrij werpen, op avontuur of hij nog iets lichten kan; krijgt hij niets terug, dan is hij van het spel af. Wie het laatste er aan blijft, heeft het spel gewonnen ; hij berooft den Arlequin van zijnen schat, en heeft daarenboven alles wat op de nummers staat tot toegift.

Manière de jouer ce jeu. Il se joue à autant de personnes que l'on voudra. L'on convient au préalable quelle sera la mise de chacun, qui devra être pour tous de même, soit 10 cents ou demi cents selon qu'on le jugera à propos. Ceci fait, l'on prend deux dés marqués de tous côtés et l'on jette à qui commencera. Le numéro que le joueur amènera au moyen des dés devra être couvert par lui avec une des pièces ci-dessus, si toutefois il ne l'est déjà ; dans ce dernier cas, il prend cette pièce ; par exemple : s'il amène 6 points et que ce numéro se trouve couvert avec un cent, alors il le prend et jette une seconde fois, jusqu'à ce qu'il amène un numéro non chargé qu'il devra couvrir avec une pièce d'argent. Si l'on amène 7, alors c'est l'Arlequin qui est le gagnant de la pièce à placer et le tout reste à la poule sans que personne puisse en prendre ou ôter quelque chose. Si longtemps qu'un des joueurs possédera des pièces, il jettera à son tour : quand il en est dénué, il peut jeter encore une fois librement afin de tâcher d'obtenir encore quelque chose, et si cela ne lui réussit pas, il perd et se trouve ainsi hors du jeu. Le dernier joueur restant gagne et dépouille l'Arlequin de son trésor et a au surplus tout ce qui se trouve sur les numéros.

Game of Harlequin. Turnhout: Brepols

late 19th century

The *Game of Seven* is known under many different names, with correspondingly different imagery. The *Game of Harlequin* looks perfectly innocuous, but the game itself is not. Here, the special rules for the throws of two or twelve are not recognized and they are treated as ordinary numbers, so that there is no quick finish to the game. The throw of seven causes money to accumulate on the central figure of Harlequin, in the usual way, but the rules say that the game continues until every player except one is completely out of money, when the last man standing takes everything. A special rule says that when a player runs out of money, one last throw is allowed for free, after which the player must leave the game.

Drink, Hansel, Drink! Germany: publisher unknown

about 1900

Schluck Hänsel , Schluck! [Drink, Hansel, Drink! – the title is given on a separate rule-sheet] is a comic variant of the *Game of Seven* with a bright chromolithographed board, included in a small compendium of German games produced about the end of the nineteenth century. The rule sheet says that the game originated 'in upper Bavaria or in the Austrian Alps', though there is no evidence for this. The 'last man standing' wins, as in the previous game but here the rules specify that each player starts with four counters only, so it is fair for everyone and becomes suitable to be played by children. The imagery of the game reflects this, decorated with brilliantly-colored characters, probably from German folk tales.

41

Game of the Pedlar. England: publisher unknown

late 19th century

Games of the 'central seven' kind were not much played in England, though a version of *the Game of the Jew* was published there early in the nineteenth century. The *Game of the Pedlar* is a rare variant. It has rules similar to those for the *Game of the Ship*, though the throw of double one is not treated specially. The rules say use two dice or a twelve-sided teetotum – but no thought has been given to what happens if the teetotum turns up a one: there is no such number on the game sheet!

THE GAME OF THE PEDLAR.

2 7 6

3 8

4 9

5 11 10

DIRECTIONS.

This Game is played either with a pair of Dice or Teetotum marked with 12 sides, & any number of persons can play. In order to decide who shall begin the game, each person throws & the highest number plays first; & the number thrown he must cover with a counter the corresponding one on the Board, each in their turn doing the same (providing it is uncovered) if it is already covered, he claims the counter on that particular number, exception is taken to N.º 7; any one throwing that number pays to "The Pedlar," which remains until one of the party throws 12 and he clears the Board, including "The Pedlar," and the game recommences.

ENTERED AT STATIONERS HALL.

Game of the Apple – New Zanzibar.

France: publisher unknown

late 19th century

The next game is a rare French version of this 'central seven' type, with an interesting name: *Game of the Apple – New Zanzibar*. In late nineteenth-century France, 'Zanzibar' was street argot for a three-dice gambling game, where three dice showing the same points evoked the cry of 'Zanzi!' by the winner, for some unknown reason. Neither is it known why it is called the *Game of the Apple*. The printed game shown here uses just two dice and has the usual rules for a Game of Seven.

Game of the Omnibus and White Ladies. France: publisher unknown

about 1830

The *Jeu des omnibus et dames blanches* [Game of the Omnibus and White Ladies} is of a different kind. The beautiful central engraving shows it being played in a fashionably-dressed company of men and women. Around this, arranged in two circles, are pictures of different horse-drawn omnibuses, numbered from 1 to 12, on which the stakes are placed. Wooden balls, also numbered from 1 to 12, are drawn from a bag to determine the winning numbers. The rules say that: 'In this game, one discovers one's character: the good player never gets upset'. Despite this wise advice, one of the players depicted is covering his face in evident horror! The game dates from the 1830s and is named for *les Dames blanches*, one of the omnibus lines that sprang up in Paris around that time. This game sheet is so elegant that, a century later, it was used as a model for the first Hermès scarf – still in production, though now with new color-ways.

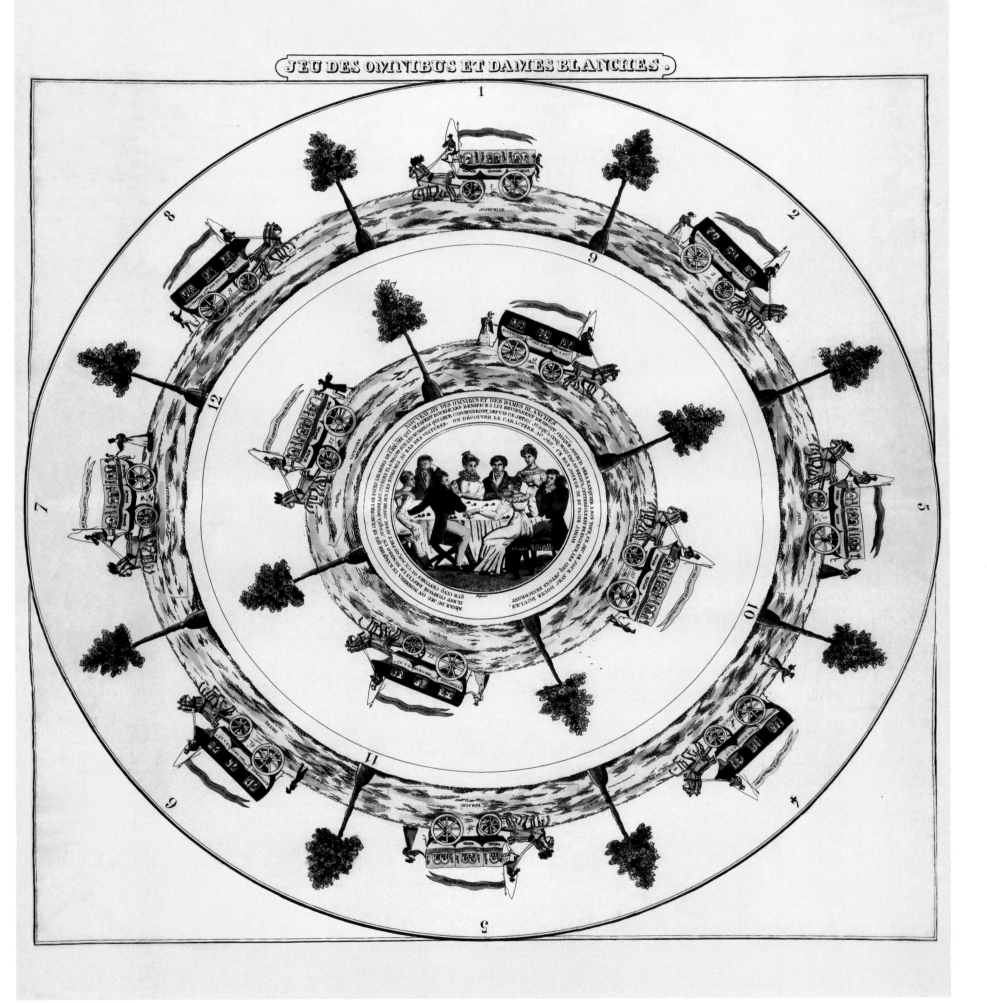

NUEVA LOTERÍA PARA NIÑOS.

La fortuna, todo lo gana. — La esgrima, ni gana ni pierde. — La equitacion, gana 2. — La gimnasia, gana 4. — La limosna, gana 10. — La devocion gana 8.

El baile, ni gana ni pierde. — El colegial, gana 2. — El cadete, gana 3. — El aprendiz, gana 1. — El escribiente gana 2. — La lectura, gana 8.

El granuja, pierde 5. — El holgazan, pierde 4. — El miedoso, pierde 1. — El monaguillo, gana 3. — El corneta, pierde 2. — El tambor, pierde 4.

El postillon, gana 8. — El pastor, ni gana ni pierde. — El lazarillo, gana 2. — El burlon, pierde 5. — El goloso, pierde 3. — El pollo, pierde 5.

El grumete, pierde 7. — El desobediente, pierde 10. — El pillete, pierde 12. — El camorrista, pierde 6. — El barquillero, pierde 4. — El arenero, pierde 2.

El limpia botas, gana 5. — El organillo, gana 2. — El lacayo, gana 4. — El fosforero, gana 3. — El hortera, gana 8. — Los núms. premiados, gana 4.

El travieso, pierde 12. — El columpio, pierde 1. — Saca el rabo, pierde 6. — Pasatiempo, ni gana ni pierde. — El compasivo, gana 20. — Cariño fraternal, gana 4.

Donde las dan las toman, p. 9. — La pedrea, pierde 8. — El premio, gana 12. — El castigo, pierde 6. — El enfermo, pierde 14. — La muerte, todo lo pierde.

EXPLICACION DEL MODO QUE SE HA DE JUGAR.—Se recortan las 48 aleluyas de este pliego, y, arrolladas, se colocan dentro de una gorra ó bolsa. Se forma un depósito de aleluyas, ó lo que se quiera jugar, por partes iguales, entre los que juegan. Cada jugador, por turno, saca una aleluya de la bolsa; si le toca una de ganar toma del fondo tantas como dice el letrero; si la saca de perder, pone las que marca la misma. Si saca la muerte, pierde tantas como haya en el depósito; y si saca la fortuna, gana todo lo del fondo, y concluye la partida, volviendo á empezar de nuevo.

MADRID.—Despacho calle de Juanelo, núm. 19

New Lottery for Children. Madrid: Despacho

about 1880

This game is another kind of lottery in which the winning and losing chances are drawn from a bag. The *Nueva Loteria per Ninos* [New Lottery for Children] is a simple sheet, printed in Madrid, showing graphic scenes of daily life that would have resonated with children. The sheet was to be cut up, separating the 48 scenes, each of which was to be rolled up and placed in the bag, from which each player would draw one in turn. The scenes have instructions as to how many stakes to pay into or take from the pool. For example, the final row reads: *donde las dan las toman* ['tit-for-tat', where a boy tormenting a horse gets kicked – pay 9]; *La pedrea* [a street fight with stones – pay 9]; *el premio* [an academic prize, showing a studious boy with his books – gain 12]; *el castigo* [punishment, showing a schoolboy crying in front of the master's desk, wearing the 'asses' ears' cap worn by dunces – pay 6]; *el enfermo* [illness – pay 14]; and finally *la muerte* [death – lose everything]. The game finishes when someone draws the first scene, the cornucopia, and takes what is left in the pool. The game sheet gives a perceptive account of life in late nineteenth-century Spain.

Educational Games: Learning for Pleasure?

First appearing in France in the seventeenth century, educational games based on the *Game of the Goose* were still popular two hundred years later, and were fun to play. But the English games of the nineteenth century, though having very beautiful images, often featured detailed instruction booklets with long passages to read out, making for a slow game and a boring experience.

Perhaps the first educational board game was the Jeu du monde *[Game of the World] designed by the map-maker Pierre Duval in 1645. It consisted of a spiral track of small vignette maps of the countries of the world. Its homage to the* Game of the Goose *was evident in that the track length was 63, the winning space representing France.*

Games designed to teach History also have their origin in mid-seventeenth-century France. The pattern is that historical events are set out chronologically along a spiral track. This strict chronological order does not give much flexibility to the designer of the game, so that these games have various different track lengths and have not much to do with the Game of the Goose.

The development of educational games came much later to England. The first surviving example is a map game from the middle of the eighteenth century, based on the Grand Tour of Europe, a journey which many wealthy young Englishmen undertook as a rite of passage into adulthood. Unlike the French geographical games, the track was set out as a zigzag of numbered points on the surface of a map. This game, the Journey through Europe, *designed by John Jefferys, had interesting rules.*

The capital cities visited ('where a king lives') acted like Goose spaces, doubling the throw. However, by the nineteenth century, the connection with the Game of the Goose had been largely forgotten in the games that then appeared.

The Georgian era was a boom time for educational games in England. The philosopher John Locke (1632-

1704) had set out his views on education in Some Thoughts Concerning Education *(1693), a manual for the education of the young sons of gentlemen. Part of Locke's philosophy involved play as an important part of the educational process. He wrote: 'None of the things they are to learn should ever be made a burthen [burden] to them.'*

From this developed the theory of learning through play – and English games manufacturers were quick to satisfy the market represented by the ever-growing affluent middle classes of the Industrial Revolution.

These games, though, were of serious purpose. They came with booklets giving detailed descriptions of the places visited in the geographic games or the events touched on in the historical games. Children found these long passages boring – and the random order in which they were consulted, as was inevitable for a dice or teetotum game, meant that learning could not be systematic.

By the Victorian era, educationalists were questioning the effectiveness of teaching through games and the choice of subjects for games began to reflect leisure pursuits rather than the strict educational curriculum – something also seen in France.

In the Netherlands, where the Game of the Goose remained popular, games for the education of younger children were developed as early as the eighteenth century, notably ABC games. There, the nineteenth century saw not only serious instructional games but also charming games with playful actions for the children, such as the game shown in this chapter, telling the story of the famous Dutch Admiral, Michael de Ruyter.

Overall, one is struck by the inventiveness of the educational game designers, often cleverly combining new ideas with the classical structures of the much older games. The attractiveness of the later games in color owes much to the development of printing techniques – and these games were often amusing and witty as well.

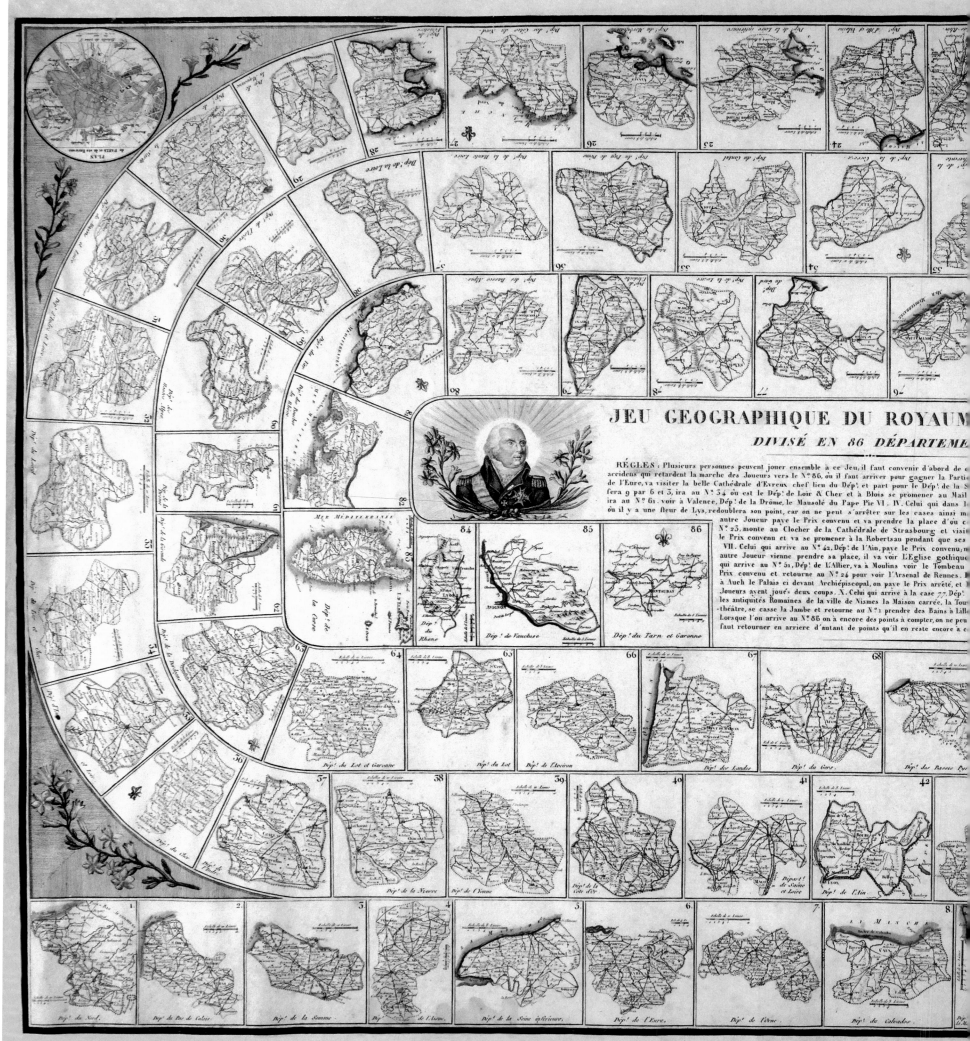

JEU GEOGRAPHIQUE DU ROYAUM[E]
DIVISÉ EN 86 DÉPARTEME[NT]

RÉGLES : Plusieurs personnes peuvent jouer ensemble à ce Jeu, il faut convenir d'abord de [?]
accidens qui retardent la marche des Joueurs vers le N°. 86, où il faut arriver pour gagner la Parti[e]
de l'Eure, va visiter la belle Cathédrale d'Evreux chef lieu du Dép'. et part pour le Dép'. de la S[?]
fera 9 par 6 et 3, ira au N°. 54 où est le Dép'. de Loir & Cher et à Blois se promener au Mail[?]
ira au N°. 61. voir à Valence, Dép'. de la Drôme, le Mausolé du Pape Pie VI . IV. Celui qui dans l[?]
où il y a une fleur de Lys, redoublera son point, car on ne peut s'arrêter sur les cases ainsi ma[?]
autre Joueur paye le Prix convenu et va prendre la place d'où ce [?]
N°. 23. monte au Clocher de la Cathédrale de Strasbourg et visi[?]
le Prix convenu et va se promener à la Robertsau pendant que ses [?]
VII. Celui qui arrive au N°. 42, Dép'. de l'Ain, paye le Prix convenu, m[?]
autre Joueur vienne prendre sa place, il va voir l'Eglise gothique [?]
qui arrive au N°. 51, Dép'. de l'Allier, va à Moulins voir le Tombeau [?]
Prix convenu et retourne au N°. 24 pour voir l'Arsenal de Rennes. [?]
à Auch le Palais ci devant Archiépiscopal, on paye le Prix arrêté, et [?]
Joueurs ayent joués deux coups. X. Celui qui arrive à la case 77. Dép'[?]
les antiquités Romaines de la ville de Nismes la Maison carrée, la Tou[?]
théâtre, se casse la Jambe et retourne au N°. 1 prendre des Bains à Lille [?]
Lorsque l'on arrive au N°. 86 on a encore des points à compter, on ne peu[?]
faut retourner en arrière d'autant de points qu'il en reste encore à c[?]

A Paris chez Basset M. d'Estampes Rue St. Jacques N°. 64

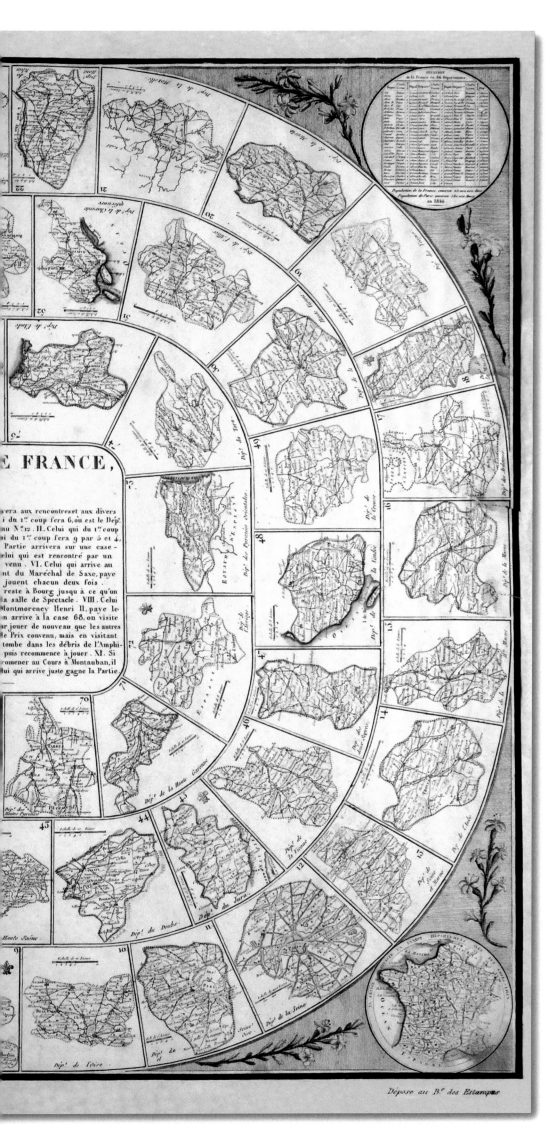

Geographical Game of the Kingdom of France.
Paris: Basset
1816

This is a direct descendant of Duval's *Game of the World*. Here, though, its spiral track consists of small maps of the Departments of France, which had replaced the old Provinces after the French Revolution of 1789. The first version of this map game appeared under the title *Geographical Game of the Republic of France* in about 1795. The version shown here is a later edition, produced in about 1816 to recognize the restoration of the Bourbon monarchy. There is now a portrait of Louis XVIII and the game's title has changed to *Geographical Game of the Kingdom of France* – in nineteenth-century France, producers of printed games had to be alert to keep up with changes of regime. The game is very clearly derived from the Game of the Goose: certain spaces are marked with a tiny *fleur-de-lys*, the badge of French royalty, to denote that they are throw-doubling spaces, like those marked with a goose in the parent game. In the original version, these spaces were marked with a tiny Gallic rooster, the symbol of the Revolution. Some of the playing instructions are amusing. At space 77, the Department of Gard, the player visits the Roman antiquities in Nismes [Nîmes] but trips over in the ruins of the amphitheater, breaks a leg and has to return to space 1, the Baths at Lille.

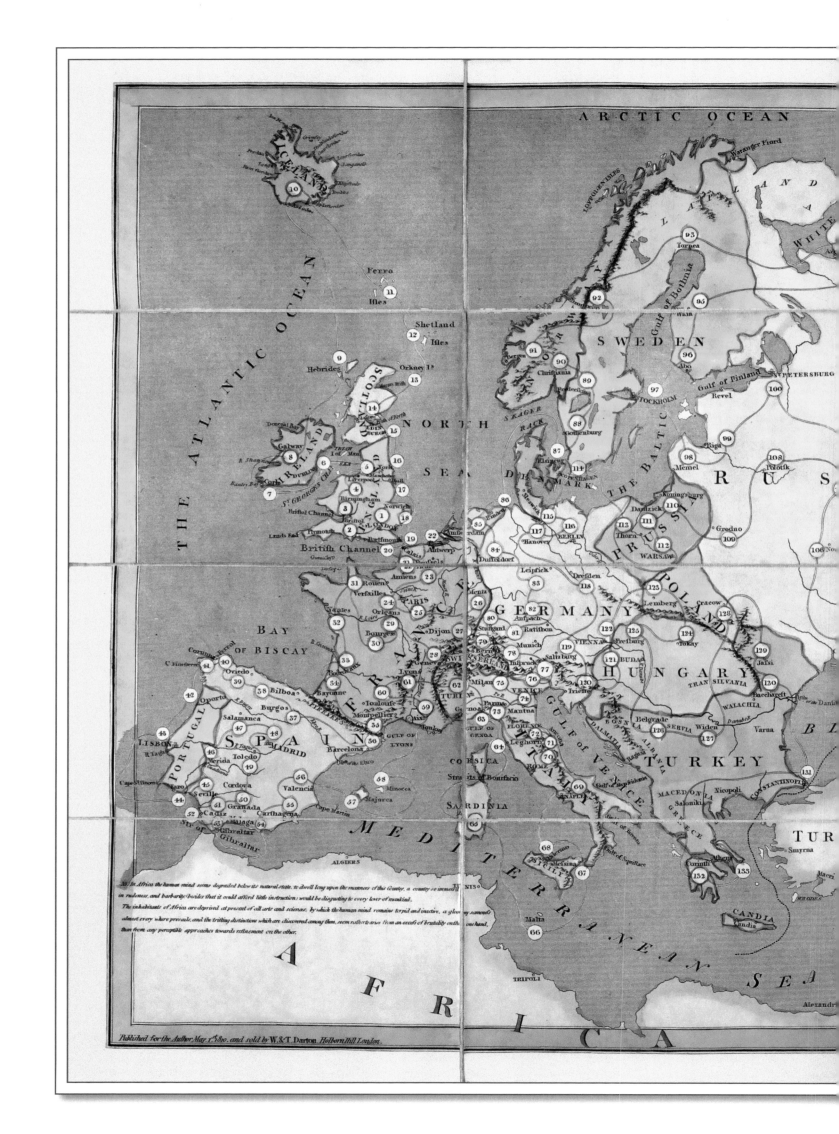

W*alker's New Geographical Game exhibiting a Tour through Europe*, dated 1810, is a complete contrast, deriving instead from John Jeffery's game of the Grand Tour. The track is set out on the face of a large map of Europe and is indicated by numbered circles representing towns and cities visited along the way, each described carefully in the booklet of 34 pages sold with the game. Some places had special instructions, though most of these were entirely unimaginative and dull: e.g., 'Paris – here wait four turns to view the city'. But, exceptionally, the city of Nantes (space 32) seems to have provoked the designer into a sharper instruction, nearly equivalent to the *death* space. 'It was here that the famous edict in favor of the Protestants was published in 1598 but in less than a century it was revoked by the celebrated Louis XIV. Here go back to no. 1, London.' Of course, Georgian London was firmly Protestant but even so the sharp irony of that word, 'celebrated', comes across. This game was published by W & T Darton and, as we shall see in the next chapter, the Dartons were not afraid of promoting their views through their games for young people.

New Historical and Chronological Game of the French Monarchy. Paris: Basset

1810

This is an historical game, showing the succession of French monarchs beginning with Clovis (c. 466-511), the first king to unite the Franks under one ruler. This game was published in Paris in 1814 to celebrate the triumphal entry of Louis XVIII into Paris, a scene shown in the central, winning space, complete with a balloon decked with flags – publishers of games liked to be up to date with technology! The track of 63 spaces clearly derives from the Game of the Goose and indeed several spaces are marked with the royal *fleur-de-lys* to denote throw-doubling spaces. The equivalent of the *death* space is (unusually) at number 57, and shows the assassination of Henri III, murdered by a Catholic fanatic in 1589. Space 31 is like the *prison* space, showing the capture and imprisonment by Hugues Capet (c. 939-996, king of the Franks from 987) of Charles, Duke of Lorraine, who had disputed the succession. These implicit references to the Game of the Goose help to make events more memorable and would have been picked up by all players of the updated game.

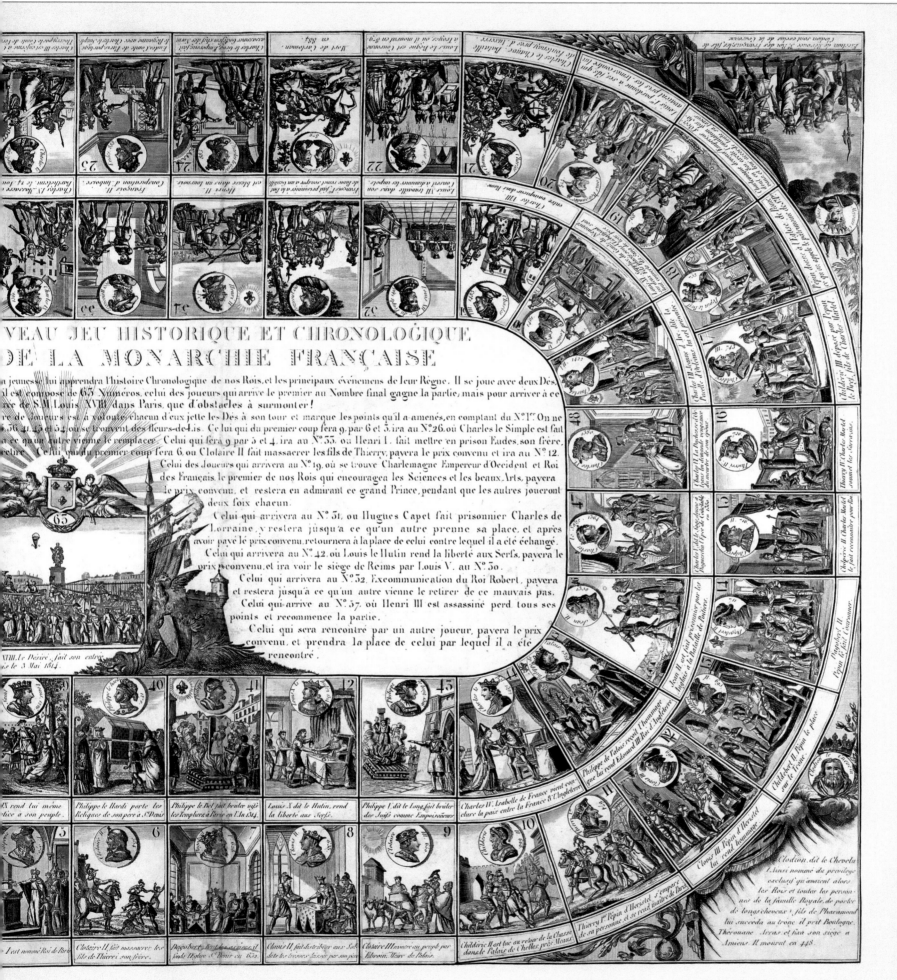

Historical Pastime. London: Passmore

1847

Games to teach History were also current in England in the nineteenth century. The earliest English example is *Historical Pastime*, published in London in 1803 by John Harris and John Wallis. It shows events in English History from the Battle of Hastings in 1066 up to the date of publication. The central space shows a portrait of the ruling monarch, George III. The game was successively updated with each change of monarch, so that the example shown, published in 1837, shows the young Queen Victoria at the center, preceded by a space referring to the abolition of slavery. The game sheet is very finely hand colored and is decorated in the four corners with battle scenes showing the British victories at Seringapatam (1799), Trafalgar (1805), Waterloo (1815), and Navarino (1827) – the effectiveness of British armed forces was being rammed home. There are special instructions for certain spaces, some of which require input from the player, contributing to the educational purposes of the game. For example, space 28 shows Roger Bacon (English philosopher of the 13th century) and has the instruction: 'Mention some discovery of this genius or pay one to the Treasury'.

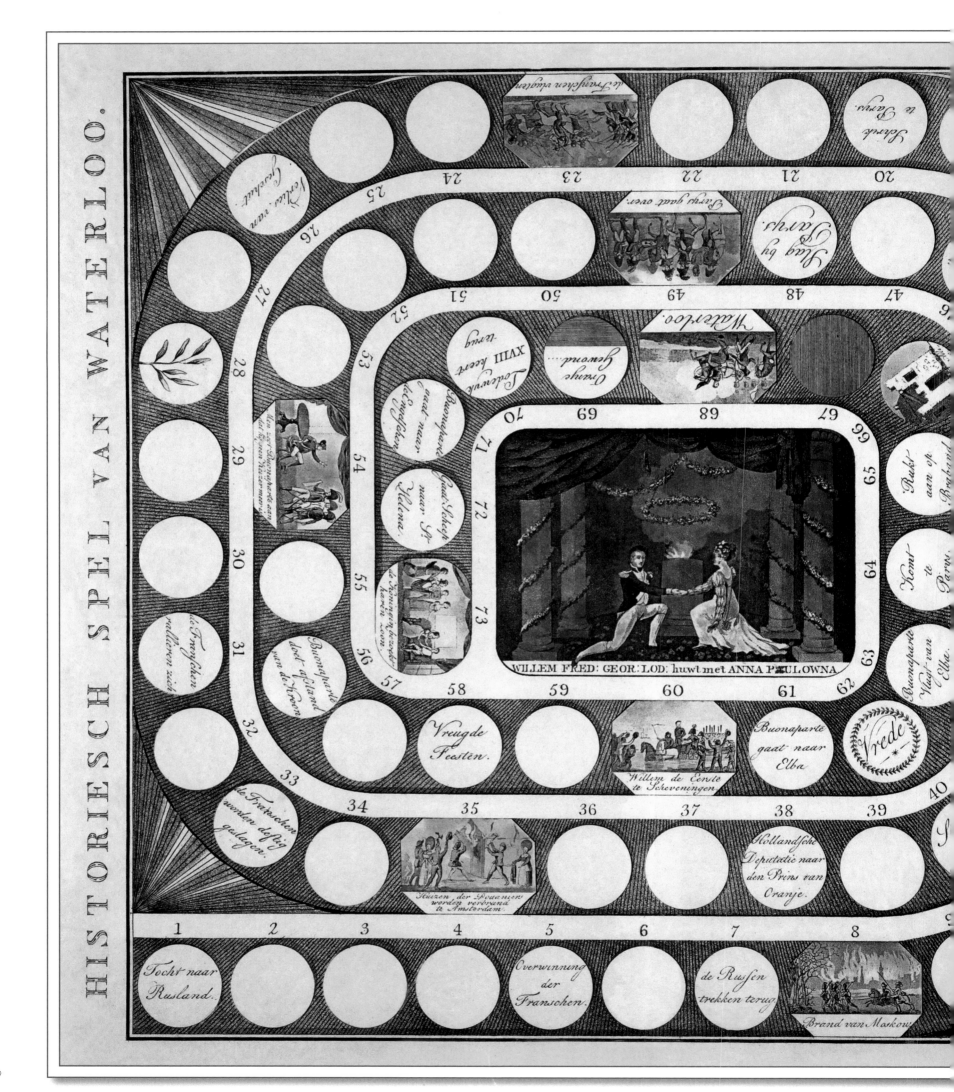

Historic Game of Waterloo.
Amsterdam: Moolenijzer
1816/1817

The Battle of Waterloo is also celebrated in the *Historisch Spel van Waterloo* [Historic Game of Waterloo] published in Amsterdam in 1816/1817. It is a finely-produced and beautiful game sheet, using a sophisticated method of etching called aquatint, a long way distant from a 'popular print'. The game sheet is accompanied by an explanatory booklet, whose introduction pulls no punches: 'The Waterloo game is intended to replace the Goose Game, from which children never learned anything, and to fix in memory for the Youth of the Netherlands the brave deeds of the people since 1812'. The central illustration forming the final space shows the betrothal of the Prince of Orange to Anna Pavlovna – they were married in St Petersburg in 1816.

De Ruyter Game.
Amsterdam: Vlieger
about 1890

Michiel de Ruyter (1607-1676) was one of the most skilful admirals in history, with several successes against the French and the English, including a daring raid on the Medway in 1667. His achievements are told in this bright chromolithographed game. It is a 63-space game, though its rules are individual, owing little to the Game of the Goose. It is cleverly designed for the amusement of children. Landing on space 2, the children must sing the de Ruyter song: *Met een blauwgeruite kiel/Draaide hij aan't grote wiel* [In a blue checkered shirt/he turned the great wheel], referring to the young Michiel at the boring work of turning the wheel in a rope factory, as shown. His feat of climbing the church tower, shown at space 3, requires the child who lands there to emulate him by standing on a chair; landing on the statue at space 17 requires the child to assume the pose illustrated and keep still for two turns. There are special rules for the splendid row of cannon along the broadside of the ship. Perhaps the scene of de Ruyter drinking his companions under the table (space 15) would nowadays be regarded as unsuitable but, overall, the game must have acquainted Dutch children with their naval heritage in an amusing and compelling way.

The Pleasures of Astronomy.
London: Wallis
1804

Instruction in science was not neglected in the nineteenth century, though there are fewer examples of games for this subject than for Geography and History. This fine English example, *The Pleasures of Astronomy*, shows at its center the original observatory at Greenwich, London, from which the prime meridian is defined. Round it are portraits of Ptolemy, Tycho Brahe, Copernicus and Sir Isaac Newton. The game was 'revised and approved by Mrs Bryan of Blackheath'. She ran a school in London and was a pioneer in science education for girls. The rule book accompanying the game, suggests that she did not spare the stupid or inattentive:

Space 6: *The County Gaol* — This is the place for those who attend more to the motions of Billiard Balls, more than to the motions of the Planets. However hard you think your case, / Stay here till someone takes your place.

Space 15: *The Man in the Moon* — It is the ridiculous idea of some ignorant people, that there is a Man in the Moon, with a Dog and a Bundle of Wood, who causes the different appearances of it by eating it away, while they say it grows back again every month. That you may know better, go back to No. 13, [The Phases of the Moon] and read to yourself the description you will find there.

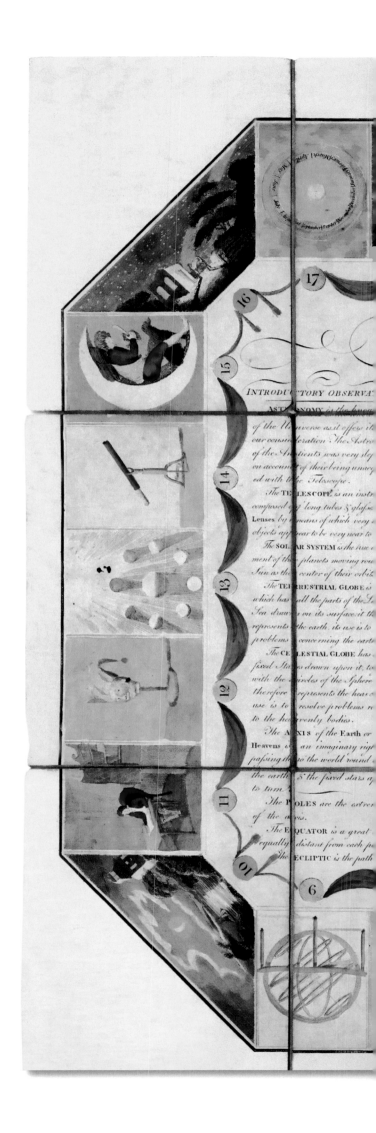

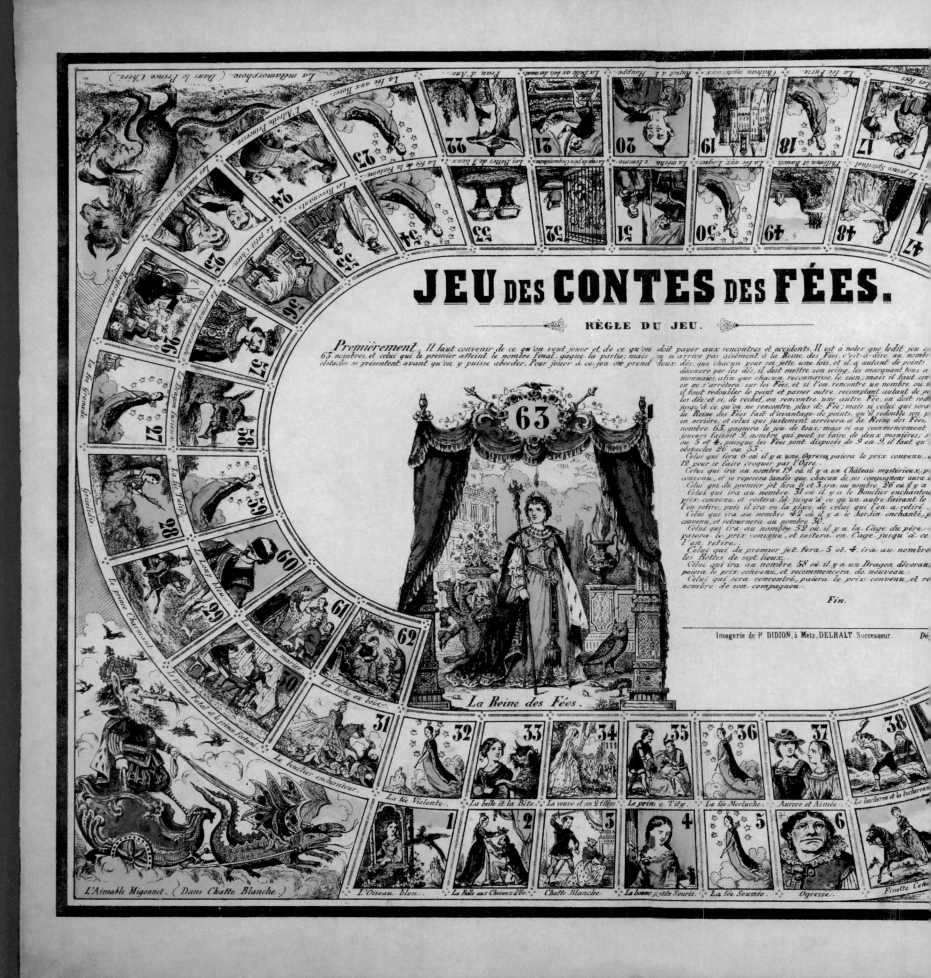

JEU DES CONTES DES FÉES.

RÈGLE DU JEU.

Premièrement, Il faut convenir de ce qu'on veut jouer et de ce qu'on doit payer aux rencontres et accidents. Il est à noter que ledit jeu est 63 nombres, et celui qui le premier atteint le nombre final, gagne la partie; mais on n'arrive pas aisément à la Reine des Fées, c'est-à-dire au nombre obstacles se présentent avant qu'on y puisse aborder. Pour jouer à ce jeu on prend deux dés, que chacun pour soi jette une fois, et il a autant de points

découvre par les dés, il doit mettre son seing, les marquant tous à
monnaie, afin que chacun reconnaisse le sien; mais il faut con
on ne s'arrêtera sur les Fées, et si l'on rencontre un nombre ou u
il faut redoubler le point et passer outre, recomptant autant de p
les dés; et si, de rechef, on rencontre une autre Fée, on doit red
jusqu'à ce qu'on ne rencontre plus de Fée; mais si celui qui sera
la Reine des Fées fait d'avantage de points, qu'il redouble son p
en arrière, et celui qui justement arrivera à la Reine des Fées,
nombre 63, gagnera le jeu de tous; mais si au commencement
pouvers laissât 9, nombre qui peut se faire de deux manières; s
ou 5 et 4, puisque les Fées sont disposés de 9 en 9, il faut qu'
obstacles 26 ou 53.

Celui qui fera 6 où il y a une Ogresse, paiera le prix convenu,
12 pour se faire croquer par l'Ogre.

Celui qui ira au nombre 19 où il y a un Château mystérieux, p
convenu, et se reposera tandis que chacun de ses compagnons aura e
Celui qui du premier jet fera 6 et 3, ira au nombre 26 où il y a
Celui qui ira au nombre 31 où il y a le Bouclier enchanteu
prix convenu, et restera là jusqu'à ce qu'un autre faisant le
l'en retire, puis il ira en la place de celui qui l'en a retiré.
Celui qui ira au nombre 43 où il y a le Jardin enchanté, p
convenu, et retournera au nombre 30.

Celui qui ira au nombre 52 où il y a la Cage du père,
paiera le prix convenu, et restera en Cage jusqu'à ce
l'en retire.

Celui qui du premier jet fera 5 et 4, ira au nombre
les Bottes de sept lieux.

Celui qui ira au nombre 58 où il y a un Dragon dévoran
paiera le prix convenu, et recommencera de nouveau.
Celui qui sera rencontré, paiera le prix convenu, et re
nombre de son compagnon.

Fin.

Imagerie de P. DIDION, à Metz, DELHALT Successeur.

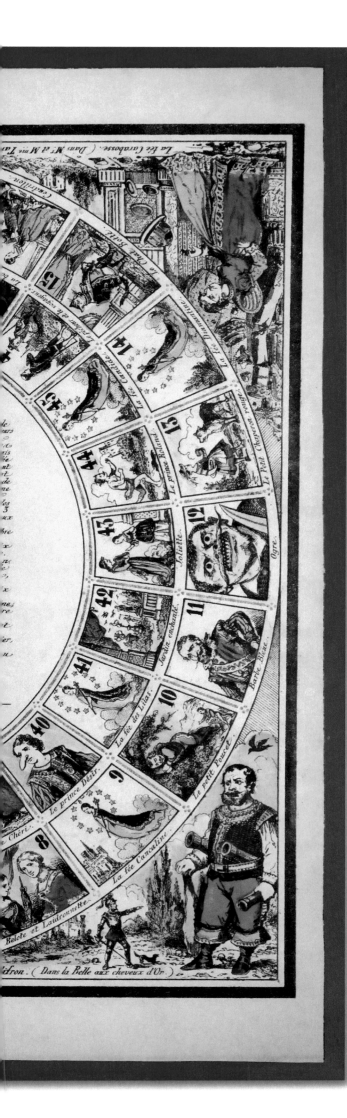

Game of Fairy Tales. Metz: Didion

late 19th century

Games were also produced to suit a younger audience. The 63 spaces of this example are filled with characters from fairy tales: the Blue Bird, the Beauty with Golden Hair, the White Cat, and so on. Fairies take the place of geese in the classic two-track series beginning on spaces 5 and 9, respectively. The hazard spaces are interpreted with some wit. Instead of the usual bridge at space 6, there is an ogress and the player must go to space 12 to be crunched up by the ogre. The *death* space at 58 shows a dragon devouring a knight (begin again!). Unusually, there is a witty treatment of the initial throw of 9: a magician takes the player to space 26 on throwing 6,3 whereas seven-league boots take the player to space 53 on throwing 5,4. This is a cheaply-produced wood engraving, with stencil color, suitable for the lower end of the juvenile market.

The Potatoes Game. Germany: publisher unknown

late 19th century

This unassuming game presents an unusual theme for education – farming potatoes! It is a simple uncolored lithograph, with title and rules in both French and German, indicating Alsace production. The rules are likewise of the simplest, being instructions to pay or take from the pool, and to advance or go back along the short, circular track of 25 spaces. The only instruction related to the imagery is that, at space 19, unloading the cart is taking so long that the player must wait until joined by another, who then takes his or her place, as in the *well* or *prison* rule. The illustrations of the various steps in growing, harvesting and eating potatoes are carefully drawn, giving instructive pictures of the equipment used and making evident the distinctions between women's and men's work. In the center, the farmer's family sits down to a meal and give thanks for their food. This game gives a real insight into the simple rural life of the time.

Das Kartoffel-Spiel.

Jeder Spieler setzt 12 Marken in die Kasse und nimmt irgend eine Sache zum Setzen. Nun wird gewürfelt. Wer zuerst nach N°3 kommt, setzt sein Zeichen auf N°1. und fängt das Spiel an. Wirst er N°4, so rückt er gleich weiter auf N°15. N°6. bezahlt 2 Marken. N°10. bekommt 5 Marken und rückt auf N°13. Wer 12. wirst, geht wieder auf N°7 zurück. N°18 bezahlt 4 Marken. Wer N°9 wirst, bekommt 6 Marken und geht weiter auf N°21. Wer nach N°19 kommt, hilft so lange den Wagen abladen bis ihn ein Anderer ablöst. In der Küche bleibt man so lange, bis man noch 3 Augen wirst, worauf man das Spiel gewonnen hat und Alles bekommt, was in der Kasse ist, und sich auf den für ihn bereit stehenden Stuhl setzt und ißt. Die Nummern 2. 5. 8. 11. 14. 17. 20. 23. zahlen alle 1. Marke Strafe. Wer über 25 wirst, geht wieder so weit zurück, als er Augen mehr hat.

Le jeu des pommes de terre.

Chaque joueur paye 12 marques dans la caisse et prend un objet quelconque pour marquer son numéro. Celui qui vient le premier, sur N°3 met sa marque sur N°1 et commence le jeu. N°4 avance toute suite sur N°15. N°6 paye 2 mq. N°10 reçoit 5 mq, et avance sur N°13. N°12 recule sur N°7. N°18 paye 4 mq. N°9 reçoit 6 mq, et avance sur N°21. N°19 aide si l'on ętemps decharger la voiture jusqu'à ce qu'autre joueurs y joigne et le remplace. Dans la cuisine, on s'arrête jusqu'à ce qu'on fait 3 points, alors on a gagné le jeu et reçoit tout ce qu'il y a dans la caisse et s'assied sur la chaise préparée et mange. Les numéros 2. 5. 8. 11. 14. 17. 20. 23. payent tous 1 mq. d'amende. Celui qui jette plus de 25 recule l'autant qu'il a fait trop de points.

Game of the End of the Century.
Paris: Saussine
1899

A beautiful and fitting conclusion to both this chapter and the nineteenth century, the *Jeu fin de siècle* [Game of the End of the Century] shows in graphic form the achievements of that inventive century. At space 1, an infant in its cradle symbolizes the new century, while the eighteenth century is symbolized by an old man carrying a sack full of outmoded inventions, like the semaphore. Each space of the track shows an invention or achievement with its appropriate date, until at space 52 a tombstone records the 'death' of the nineteenth century, requiring a fresh start. The delightful winning space in the center looks forward to the century to come: 'Embark here for Paris to Marseilles in 5 minutes' in a wondrous flying machine. The *Tour Eiffel* is dwarfed by a huge rival, and a bridge of great length reaches across the Channel. The blue numbers on the track indicate the 'goose' spaces, where the throw is doubled. The white numbers lead to a succession of disciplines, where the player must advance step by step, until he or she rejoins the game at the *Expo. Universelle 1889*, 'to make use of all they have learned'. The drawings include exact representations of the costumes of the time, so great care has been taken to provide a correct 'feel' for the period.

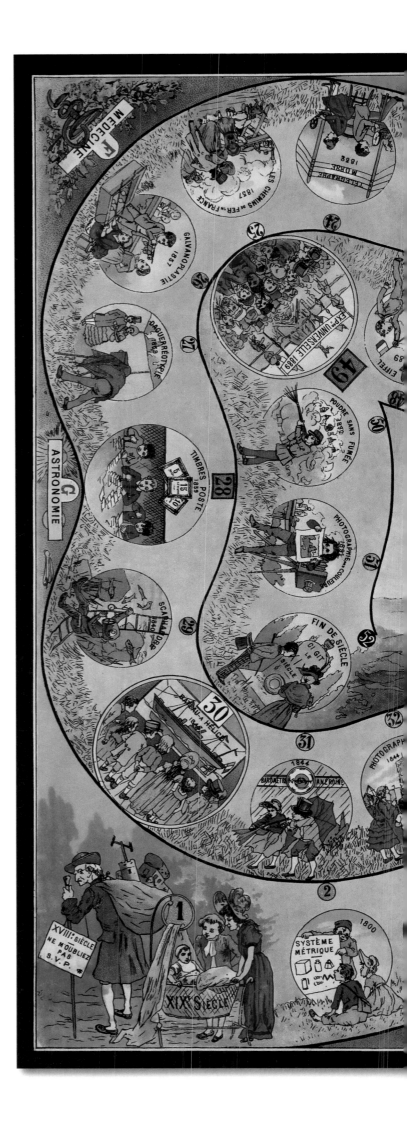

Morals and Religion: How to Behave!

In England, games for the moral education of young people were available in great variety. Even games that did not have an overtly moral theme could be hijacked for the purpose. France, by contrast, produced games on religious and spiritual themes.

Although in eighteenth-century France educational games were in full swing, the vogue for such games in England did not begin until the very end of the century. Arguably, the game that triggered this off was itself an import - actually a pirated copy of a French game, the New Game of Human Life, *which fittingly begins this chapter. It was a game with a distinct moral flavor and was highly influential. Within a couple of decades after the turn of the century, all the main English producers of games had jumped on the bandwagon and upwards of a dozen different games for 'moral improvement' were available, as well as many other kinds of printed games. They were expensive productions, finely engraved and hand-colored – usually by children pressed into work, sitting in a circle, each one specializing in painting a particular color with the finest of brushes, and*

passing the game sheet from hand to hand.

The cost (around seven shillings) of one of these English games, elaborately presented in a mahogany box with teetotum and 'pillars' (colored wooden pawns to act as tokens marking a player's place on the game sheet), could easily represent a good fraction of a week's wage for a skilled craftsman. These, then, were up-market games, sold in low numbers. Today, they are some of the rarest games on the market. Much sought by collectors, some of them survive in only a handful of examples, these being almost impossible to find complete with their rule-books and playing apparatus, even in museum collections.

The English games sometimes claimed moral virtue for supplying a teetotum rather than dice. For example, a footnote on the New Game of Human Life says: 'It is necessary to inform the Purchaser the Totum must be marked with the Figures 1 2 3 4 5 6 & to avoid introducing a Dice Box into private Families, each player must spin twice, which will answer the same purpose.' But a more prosaic reason for supplying an unmarked teetotum was to avoid the extremely high duty on dice in Georgian England: for double dice, this would have been 20 shillings – more than twice the cost of the game.

A common feature of the moral games was to encourage charitable giving and good works among the poor, giving support to the contention that these games were aimed squarely at an affluent upper-class market. It was felt important to inculcate the habit of giving, even from a young age, when as little as a penny might be afforded. A particular feature of English games, especially those produced by publishers from Quaker families, was that moral overtones were often imported into games whose themes would appear to be quite matter-of-fact. Thus, even the behavior of birds could be invoked to teach a moral lesson, while a look round London at its public buildings could produce reflections on the ill effects of the Colonial system and the East India Company, as well as on the real value of money. Some of these English moral games were deadly serious and would scarcely have enlivened even a wet weekend. Others, though, were more sympathetically designed to amuse children, while not forgetting that a moral lesson was to be conveyed during play.

In France, a predominantly Roman Catholic country, games with a spiritual focus were preferred. Some of these were directly intended to instruct children going into religious foundations while others were for more general consumption, such as the Moral and Instructive game shown here. They often dealt in some detail with the various categories of sin, calling for repentance and the embracing of particular virtues to counteract them. A number of these games were curiously matter-of-fact about religious symbols – an example (not shown here) is a game where the Stations of the Cross become the Goose spaces doubling the throw. The games in this chapter throw into sharp contrast the attitudes to religion in England and in France.

The chapter concludes with the charming Willy's Walk to see Grandmamma. Here there are no deep moral or spiritual insights – just good behavior and kindness to others.

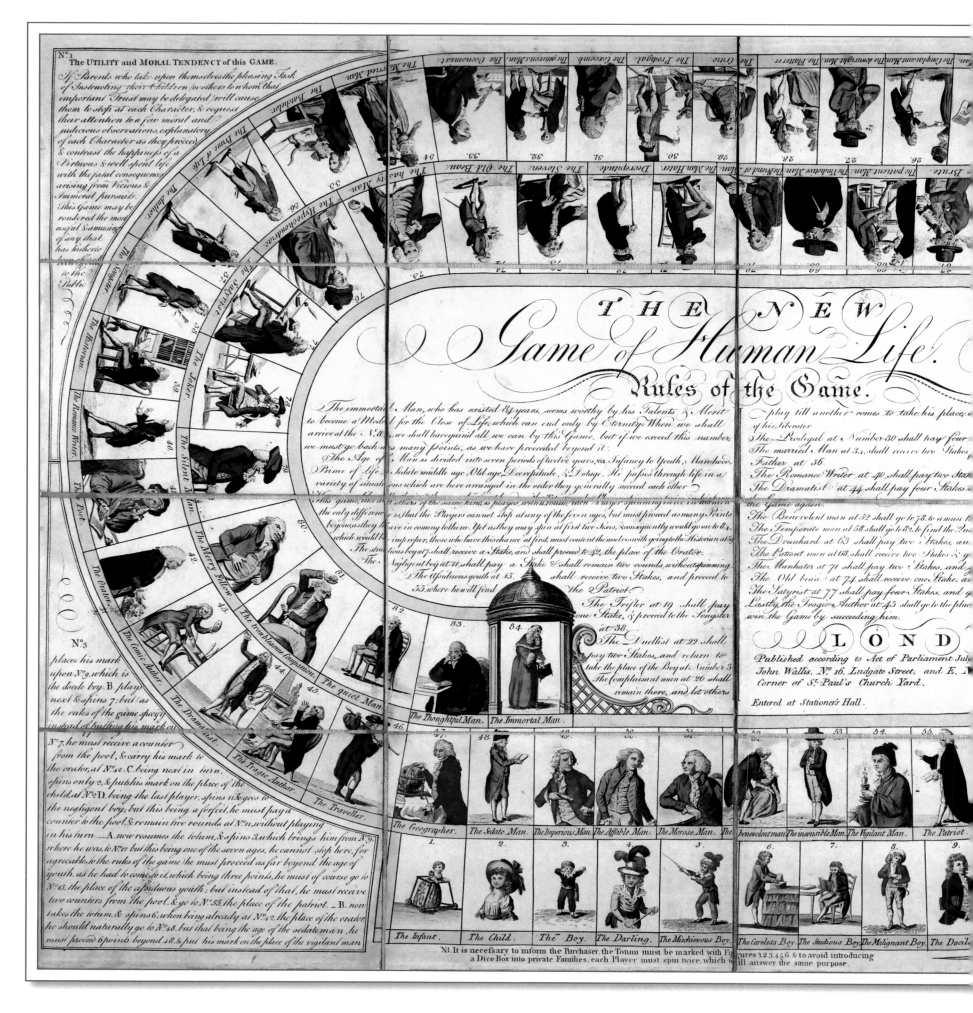

The New Game of Human Life.
London: Newbery and Wallis

1790

The *New Game of Human Life* is a version of the Game of the Goose extended to 84 spaces, so as to represent the seven ages of man, each of 12 years. The 'age' spaces, numbered 12, 24 etc act as Goose spaces, doubling the throw. Its claim to being a 'moral' game rests on the various hazard spaces. For example, the *Prodigal* at space 30 must pay four stakes and return to space 6, the *Careless Boy*. Sure enough, the Prodigal is pictured throwing away his money, while the Careless Boy is building a house of cards – a metaphor for wasted effort. The publishers were Elizabeth Newbery and John Wallis. She was a leading publisher of juvenile material and probably was responsible for the high claim to the 'Utility and Moral Tendency of this Game' that appears at the upper left. The game itself is a close copy of a game published by Crépy in Paris fifteen years earlier – but changes have been made for the English market. The figure at the winning space becomes Sir Isaac Newton, instead of the more controversial figure of Voltaire in the French version. A gross caricature of George, Prince Regent, appears at space 57, labeled the *Ambitious Man*, while Captain Cook, the explorer, is shown with his globe at space 47 as the Geographer.

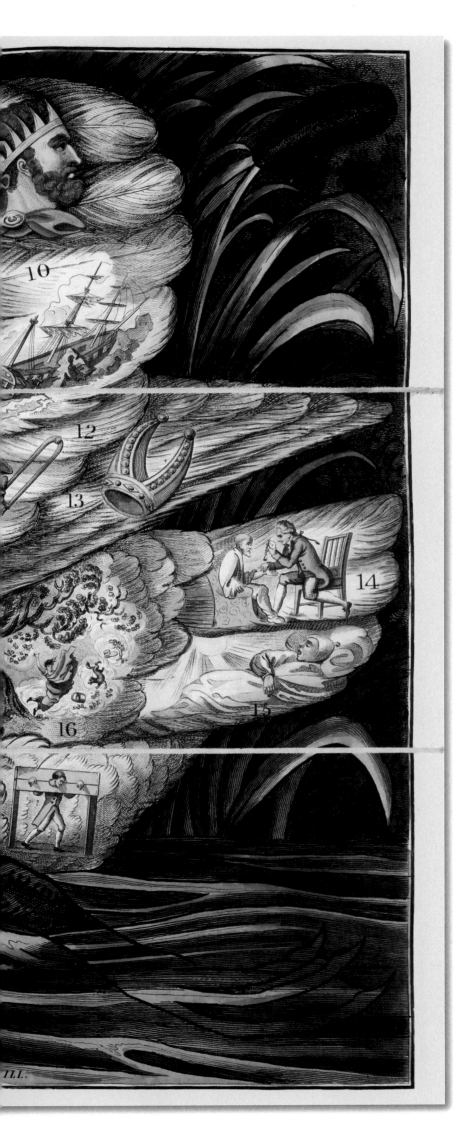

The Noble Game of the Swan.

London: Darton

1821

The next example is a fine Darton engraving, beautifully colored by hand: *The Noble Game of the Swan – containing amusement and instruction for all ages and sizes*. But the subjects depicted form a bizarre range indeed. The track starts by showing a key-stone, a post-horse, a museum, a merchant, a woolpack, a jockey and an abbey – no obvious connections here. The booklet accompanying the game gives descriptions of each subject, often of a patriotic nature, for example (of space 5): 'Wool forms the principal branch of our trade with other countries and the English woollen cloths have no competitor.' Morals come in at space 15, the sluggard: 'What can be said in favor of this personage, whose very name excites contempt?' But perhaps the clearest moral lesson is that the booklet also contains a caution against cheating by moving the teetotum or the counter!

The Novel and Elegant Game
of the Basket of Fruit.
London: Darton
1845

Darton's *Game of the Basket of Fruit*, though very beautiful in design, offers a chaotic range of subjects. The scenes are: 1. Penitentiary, 2. Trial by Jury, 3. Domiciliary Visit to the Indigent, 4. Students at the Royal Academy, 5. Exhibition at the Royal Academy, 6. An Infirmary, 7. An Alms House, 8. A Lecture on Chemistry, 9. A Blue-coat Boy, 10. A National School, 11. Confirmation, 12. A Bazaar, 13. Greenwich Pensioners, 14. Female Benevolent Society, 15. School for the Blind, 16. Chelsea Pensioners, 17. Matrimony, 18. Harvest Home, 19. A Bible Society, 20. Glory inciting an Oxonian and a Cantab student to Emulation, Learning and the Arts.

The Dartons were Quakers and the descriptions of the various scenes in the accompanying booklet include expressions of their beliefs and philosophies. For example, the note describing the Female Benevolent Society procession shows the Quakers' dislike of public display: '... we are tempted to think that these good ladies would look to more advantage seated in conversation for the good of the society than thus parading the streets with painted flags.' This would not have been a jolly game to play!

The Swan of Elegance. London: Harris

1814

By comparison with the preceding Darton games, *The Swan of Elegance* published by John Harris is an altogether jollier affair. Scenes of children behaving well or behaving badly are set out along a crimson ribbon ornamenting a wonderful swan. For each scene, there is a moralizing verse in the accompanying booklet. Space 23 shows *Gluttonous Helen* — 'Here's Helen near choking with eating mince pies, / What a shame, she so greedy should be; / She must go back to Charles a lesson to learn, / And deposit in bank counters three.' And indeed, on space 9, we see 'Frugal Charles' cutting a very thin slice from a large iced cake. Space 10 shows False Harriot, who has broken a dish but is trying to blame the cat. The attempted deceit does her no good: she has to pay four counters to the bank and miss three turns.

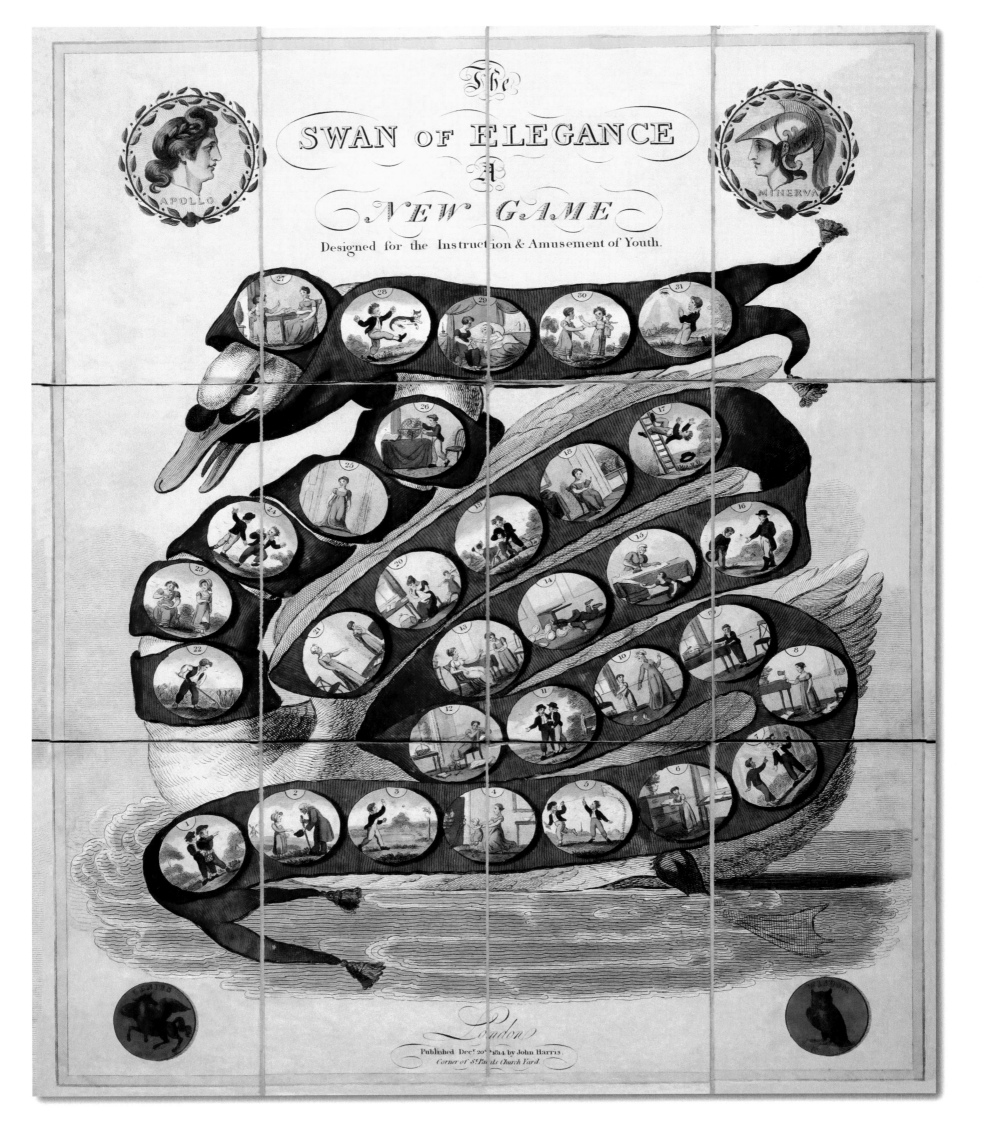

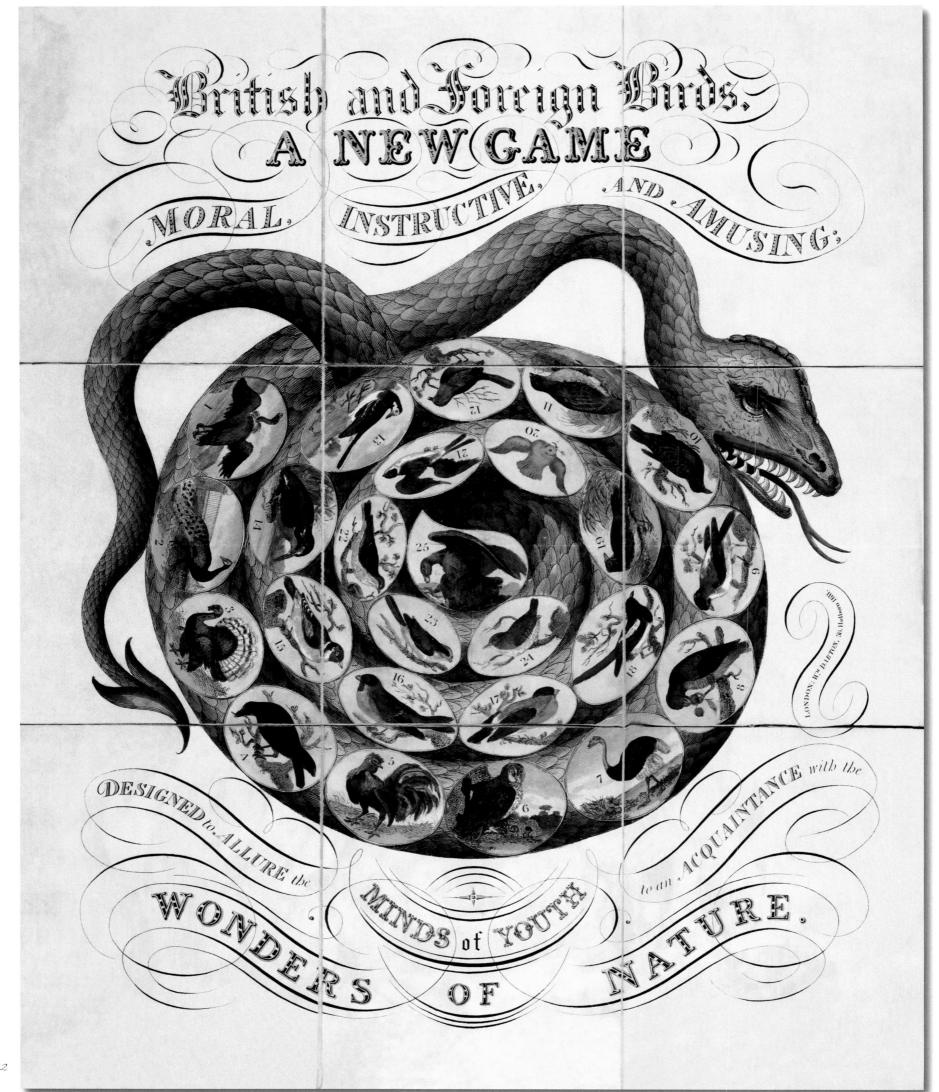

British and Foreign Birds. London: Darton

1820

'A NEW GAME MORAL INSTRUCTIVE AND AMUSING DESIGNED to ALLURE the MINDS of YOUTH to an ACQUAINTANCE with the WONDERS OF NATURE' – so claims in fine bombastic style the sub-title of the Darton game of *British and Foreign Birds*. The engraved playing track consists of 25 spaces, each depicting a bird. These are connected by the body of an impressive snake, with forked tail, forked tongue and a menacing set of curved teeth. What effect this fearsome decoration had on the 'minds of youth' is not recorded – it certainly has nothing to do with the game itself. The rule booklet devotes a separate page to each bird, the intention being that the player should refer to this for a description, so the pace of the game must have been slow. For a few of the spaces, instructions are given that are thought to reflect the character of the bird and thereby to point up a moral lesson. Space 2: *The Peacock* — stop one turn to view the beautiful plumage of this bird, and to ridicule its vanity. Space 7: *The Ostrich* — the spinner cannot keep pace with the ostrich; therefore spin again. Space 8: *The Parrot* — let the player go back three turns, for prating so much. The Eagle, 'that majestic and distinguished bird', dignifies the winning space.

A Survey of London by a Party of Tarry-at-Home Travelers.

London: Darton

1820

How on Earth can a game about the public buildings of London be used to impress moral values? Such was not beyond the power of the Dartons in their game, *A Survey of London by a Party of Tarry-at-Home Travelers*. Their Quaker values are shown to the full in the booklet, which contains long descriptions of the seventeen buildings depicted. A visit to the Mint (space 12) elicits the comment: 'The sight of such riches may create wonder; but it should be remembered that wealth has its cares' and goes on to 'advise my young friends' that their New-year's shilling [a usual gift for children in well-to-do families], worth twelve pence, should be used to provide 'a scanty meal' for the same number of destitute and starving creatures. But the strongest moral force of the booklet is reserved for the East India Company, whose museum is at space 7 and displays many objects taken from their original owners: 'We might have spared the thousands of eastern natives who have suffered from our false ambition and unjust claims on their property and landed possessions'. Such frank anti-colonial attitudes were rare in Georgian London.

Moral and Instructive Game. Nancy: Jarville

about 1890

This 'moral and instructive' French game is in fact a religious game. It dates from about 1860, though the example shown is a reprint made towards the end of the century. Its 63-space track culminates in Paradise, showing God the Father flanked by images of the Blessed Virgin Mary and of Jesus. The hazard spaces correspond to various sins. The capital sins offer the player a choice between paying a stake to the pool or returning to the corresponding virtue to which the sin is opposed – a rare example of choice of move being allowed in a game of the Goose type. Landing on other virtues doubles the throw, as for a goose space. Other sins involve penalties familiar in the parent game. As always with such games, it is interesting to see how the *death* space is treated. Here it is Pride (suffering a fall on space 58), with the usual rule 'begin again'. Strangely, the designer of the game has forgotten to give a rule for the sin of Envy, graphically shown at space 44 as one man beating another savagely with a club. Otherwise, the designer has chosen to fill the non-active spaces with images of country trades and occupations, which sit rather innocently against the intensity of the spiritual scenes depicted elsewhere.

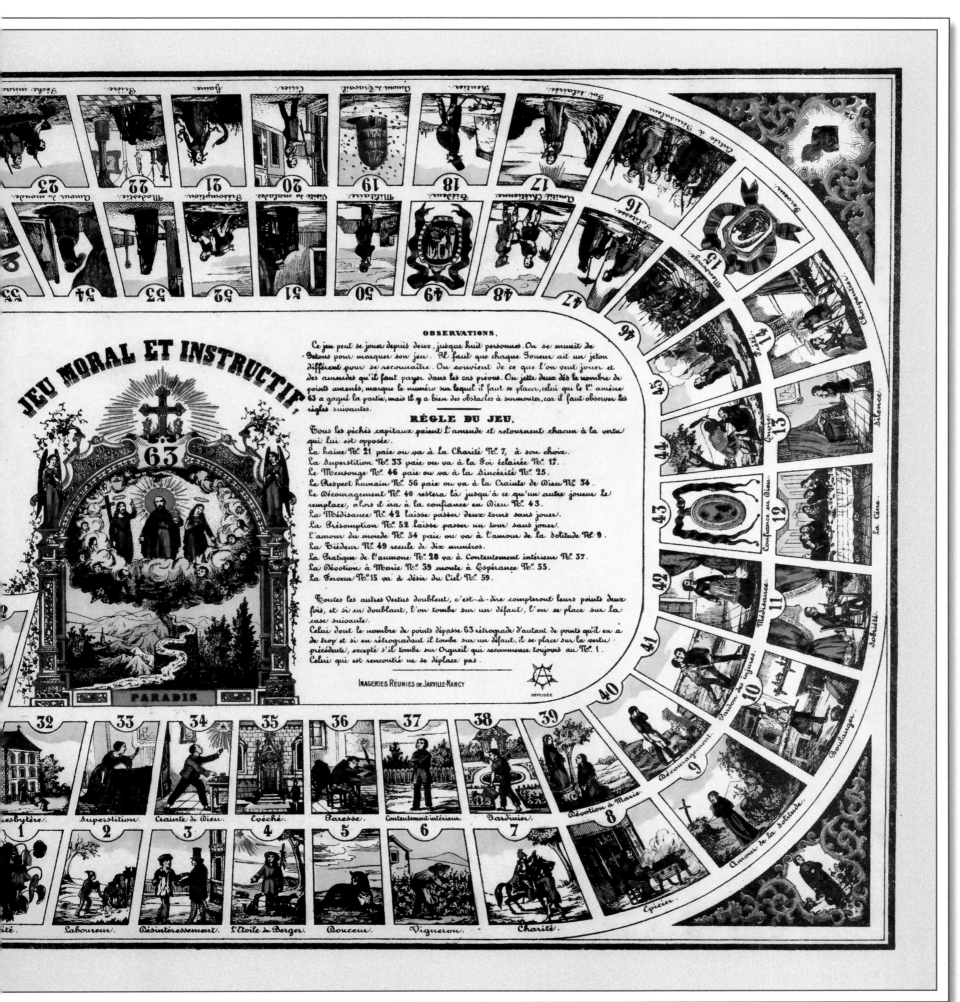

Willy's Walk to see Grandmamma.

London: Myers

1869

Willy's Walk to see Grandmamma is a light-hearted game to amuse children. It has a 79-space track, with Grandmamma's house at the center. This game dates from 1869, half a century after the serious and 'improving' games like those of the Dartons. Here, the accidents on the journey are not threatening and the moral lessons are implied, rather than drawn explicitly. Some of the hazards resemble those of the Goose game. At space 20, Willy falls down and must wait for someone to pick him up, or miss two turns. Other spaces indicate realistically how a young boy might waste time on a journey – buying apples, picking flowers, forgetting his parcel so that he must go back, joining in a game of marbles and so on. On the other hand, begging a ride in the baker's cart, or catching the omnibus, takes him forward more quickly. Interestingly, when Willy does a moral action, such as giving a poor child an apple or persuading some boys not to tease a dog, he has to miss a turn or two. In the earlier games, the opportunity to point a moral by giving him some advantage for his good behavior would not have been lost.

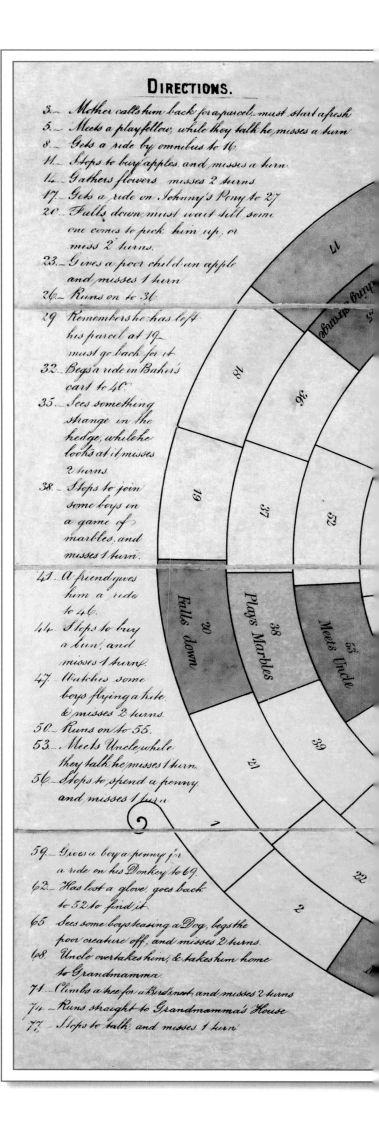

DIRECTIONS.

3.– Mother calls him back for a parcel, must start afresh

5.– Meets a playfellow, while they talk he misses a turn

8.– Gets a ride by omnibus to 16.

11.– Stops to buy apples, and misses a turn

14.– Gathers flowers, misses 2 turns.

17.– Gets a ride on Johnny's Pony to 27

20.– Falls down, must wait till some one comes to pick him up, or miss 2 turns.

23.– Gives a poor child an apple and misses 1 turn

26.– Runs on to 36.

29.– Remembers he has left his parcel at 19– must go back for it

32.– Begs a ride in Baker's cart to 40.

35.– Sees something strange in the hedge, while he looks at it misses 2 turns.

38.– Stops to join some boys in a game of marbles, and misses 1 turn.

41.– A friend gives him a ride to 46.

44.– Stops to buy a bun, and misses 1 turn.

47.– Watches some boys flying a kite & misses 2 turns.

50.– Runs on to 55.

53.– Meets Uncle while they talk he misses 1 turn.

56.– Stops to spend a penny and misses 1 turn.

59.– Gives a boy a penny for a ride on his Donkey to 69

62.– Has lost a glove, goes back to 52 to find it.

65.– Sees some boys teasing a Dog, begs the poor creature off, and misses 2 turns.

68.– Uncle overtakes him, & takes him home to Grandmamma

71.– Climbs a tree for a Birds nest, and misses 2 turns

74.– Runs straight to Grandmamma's House

77.– Stops to talk, and misses 1 turn

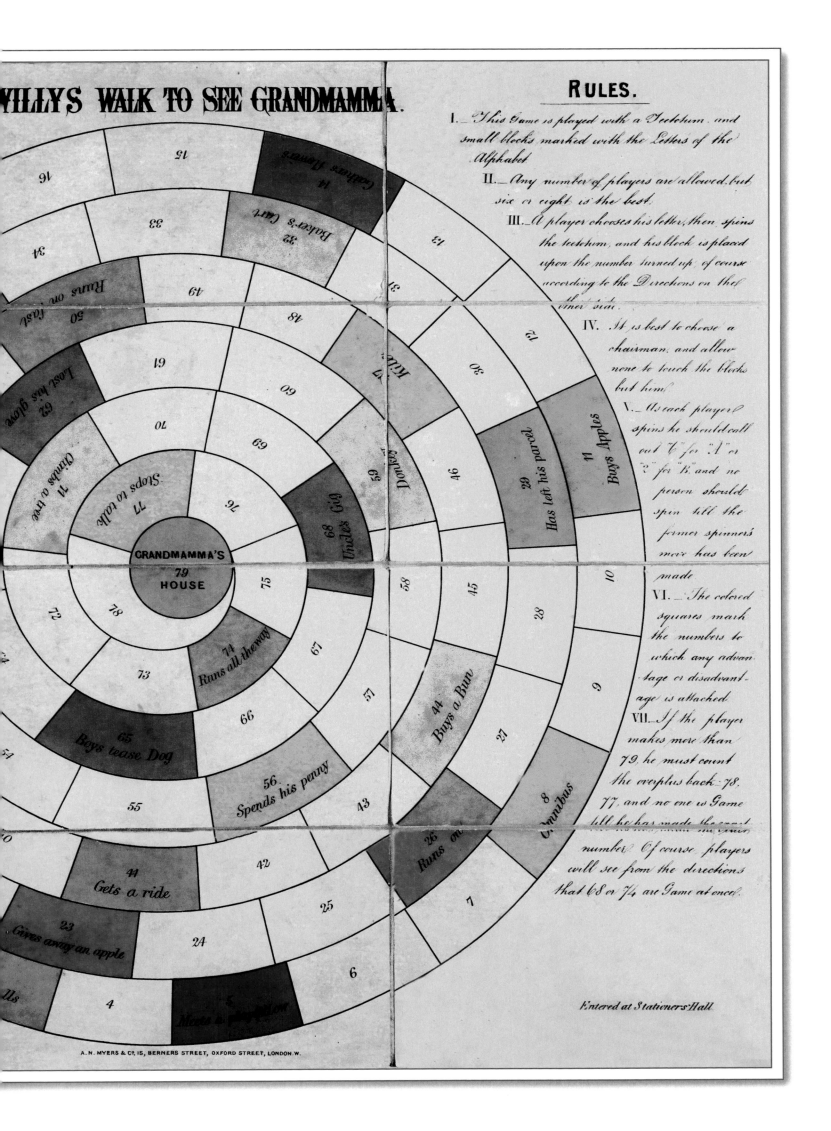

WILLYS WALK TO SEE GRANDMAMMA.

Board spaces (as labelled):
- 15
- 16
- 14 Gathers flowers
- 33
- 34
- 32 Baker's Cart
- Runs on fast
- 49
- 13
- 50
- 48
- 31
- 61
- 19
- 12
- 62 Lost his glove
- 60
- 30
- 70
- 71 Climbs a tree
- 59 Donkey
- 46
- 29 Has left his parcel
- 11 Buys Apples
- 77 Stops to talk
- 76
- 68 Gig
- 69
- 58
- 10
- Uncles
- GRANDMAMMA'S 79 HOUSE
- 75
- 45
- 28
- 72
- 78
- 67
- 9
- 74 Runs all the way
- 73
- 57
- 44 Buys a Bun
- 27
- 66
- 65 Boys tease Dog
- 56 Spends his penny
- 43
- 8 Omnibus
- 55
- 26 Runs on
- 54
- 44 Gets a ride
- 42
- 25
- 7
- 23 Gives away an apple
- 24
- 6
- 4
- 5 Meets a ...fellow
- lls

A. N. MYERS & Cº. 15, BERNERS STREET, OXFORD STREET, LONDON. W.

RULES.

I.—This Game is played with a Teetotum, and small blocks marked with the Letters of the Alphabet.

II.—Any number of players are allowed, but six or eight is the best.

III.—A player chooses his letter, then spins the teetotum, and his block is placed upon the number turned up, of course according to the Directions on the other side.

IV.—It is best to choose a chairman, and allow none to touch the blocks but him.

V.—As each player spins he should call out "Y" for "A" or "B" for "B," and no person should spin till the former spinner's move has been made.

VI.—The colored squares mark the numbers to which any advantage or disadvantage is attached.

VII.—If the player makes more than 79, he must count the overplus back—78, 77, and no one is Game till he has made the exact number. Of course players will see from the directions that 68 or 74 are Game at once.

Entered at Stationers' Hall.

Journeys: Where Shall We Go?

Journey games were especially popular in Germany, beginning with the stagecoach but updated with trains and steamships later in the century. The eighteenth-century English games based on a map of the Grand Tour of Europe were developed in the nineteenth into voyages around the World.

The Game of the Goose can be regarded as symbolizing a journey through life but the journeys in this chapter, though conducted in the imagination, are concerned with travel from place to place. The earliest is an example of the Post and Journey Game, *which originated in Germany in the late eighteenth century. In these games, the journey by horse-drawn carriage ends at the city depicted in the center, having overcome the many hazards to be expected in that era of difficult travel. These games have their own rules, rather than being direct adaptations of the Game of the Goose, though they are similar in many respects at a generic level. They have favorable spaces that move the traveler forwards and a wide range of hazards that impede progress. The rules are often cleverly written to correspond as closely as possible to the delays and frustrations of a real-life journey. And, like the Game of the Goose, they are dice games without choice of move.*

A fascination with evolving means of transport in the nineteenth century resulted in games that were devoted to particular innovations, such as the steam ferry or the railway train. Often these games were highly specific, in recording journeys from and to named places, and would have been designed to please a local audience. Some of these games were innovative in their rules, aiming to give an idea of the experience of travel by new forms of transport. Others concentrated on the technical side, for example by showing the different kinds of rolling stock on the railways, or by showing track-side equipment, stations and other railway buildings. Games of this kind can be useful to the historian because the depictions are often done with great care.

A different genre of journey games encompasses those where the places to be visited are the main theme. These can be, for example, the public buildings of a city, or the important stopping places on a longer journey. These games are the descendants of the geographical games discussed in Chapter 3. An obvious theme for such a game is a voyage around the World. Such games date from the very beginning of the nineteenth century but a particular stimulus for them was the appearance in 1873 of the novel by Jules Verne, Round the World in Eighty Days. *This resulted not only in games that showed the fictional journey of Phileas Fogg but also in games representing real journeys around the World, such as were becoming available through travel companies to satisfy the developing enthusiasm for tourism. But journeys wholly in the imagination were not forgotten – why not go to the stars via a board game?*

The journey games in this chapter include examples of a wide variety of production techniques. The Traveler in Europe *game, printed from a copper plate with beautifully detailed engraving, is typical of the Parisian printing houses that provided games for the sons of the aristocracy in a previous century. Contrast this with the cheap woodcut, on flimsy paper, of the Dutch* Steamboat *game. Both were produced in the earlier part of the nineteenth century but they address quite different markets. Around the middle of the century, lithography (printing from flat stones drawn on with greasy ink) begins to replace engraving. The game of* The Orient *shows what superb – but expensive – results can be achieved when this technique is combined with meticulous hand color. Then, towards the end of the century, printing in colors from lithographic stones – chromolithography – makes it possible to achieve both splendid game sheets like that of* Round the World in Eighty Days *and inexpensive sheets like that of the* Italian World Tour.

New Post and Journey Game. Nuremberg: Campe

about 1820

We begin with a *New Post and Journey* game dating from about 1820, produced in Nuremberg, Germany – a city which would become highly important in the production of toys and games for world markets. The first space shows the stagecoach setting off on its journey towards the central destination, the walled city on the river, which could well be a representation of Nuremberg on the River Pegnitz. Unlike the Game of the Goose, there are no throw-doubling spaces but instead the journey is divided into stages, with a station at every tenth space: landing at such a station, the player advances to the next. There is an equivalent of the death space found in the Goose game: at space 37, the coach meets with an accident and the player must start again. This game has a distinctive water hazard at space 53 which acts as a barrier. If the player lands here without having first taken the 'boat' at space 51, he or she loses the game. Points overthrown beyond 53 are counted backwards and the player cannot proceed further without having first visited the boat space. This ingenious adaptation of the finishing rule in the Goose game adds an extra touch of reality to the supposed journey.

Neues Post = u. Reise = Spiel.

1. 2. 3. 4. 5. 6. 7. 8. 9.

28. 29. 30. Station. 31. 32. 33. 34. 35. 10. Station.

27. 48. 49. 50. Station. 51. 52. 53. 36. 11.

26. 47. 60. Station. 61. 54. 37. 12.

25. 46. 59. 55. 38. 13.

24. 45. 58. 57. 56. 55. 38. 13.

23. 44. 43. 42. 41. 40. Station. 39. 14.

22. 21. 20. Station. 19. 18. 17. 16. 15.

Zum Anfang zahlt jeder 24 Marquen Postgeld, und steigt bey No 1. in den Reisewagen. Kommt man auf eine Station, so setzt man sein Zeichen auf die nächste. Wenn man in ein Wirthshaus kommt, so muß man 4 Marg. Zeche bezahlen. Bey No 3. dem Schlagbaum, kostet es 2 Marg. Weggeld. Der Meilenzeiger No 7. gewinnt 3 Marg. Die Allee No 9. gewinnt 4. Der Berg No 13. verl. 2 Marg. Die Wiese No 16. gewinnt 3 Marg. Das Dorf No 18. gewinnt 4 Marg. Der Wald No 21. verliert 3 Marg. Der Räuber No 23. plündert ein 12 Marg. Dem Bettler No 27. giebt man 1 Marg. Das Posthorn No 31. gewinnt 6 Marg. In der Mühle No 33. zahlt man fürs Nachtquartier 3 Marg. Zerbricht der Wagen No 37. so muß man wieder von vorn anfangen. Bey der Brücke No 42. giebt man 2 Marg. Zoll. Das Kornfeld No 44. gew. 5 Marg. Die Ritterburg No 47. verliert 3 Marg. Wer in die Überschwemmung geräth, ohne vorher in den Kahn No 51. sich gesetzt zu haben, ersäuft, und hat das Spiel verloren, fällt aber der Wurf darüber, so zählt man das Uebrige von No 53. zurück, bis man endlich in den Kahn kommt, und nur dann kann man weiter reisen. In dem Kloster No 57. opfert man 2 Marquen. Der Postillon No 59. erhält 8 Marquen Trinkgeld. Derjenige so am ersten in der Hauptstadt No 61. anlangt, ist Gewinner des ganzen Spiels.

Railway and Steamship Game.
Stuttgart: Hoffmann
about 1850

The *Railway and Steamship* game is a mid-century update of the Post and Journey game. The 85-space rectangular track, with rules written in each space, has as its goal a happy arrival at the railway station. But the journey is not at first mechanized and the means of transport are much like those of the earlier game. The main interest for the modern reader is in the vignettes of everyday life - for example, at space 17, showing how the account is kept at the inn on a slate. An unwelcome event is the highway robbery at space 27, where 6 stakes must be paid and the traveler must return to the preceding town. He misses the train at space 46 but catches it one space later. At space 54, walking again, he finds a hole in his boots and has to have them mended. But at space 58, the traveler arrives at a harbor and, at the next space, crosses a perilous gangplank to board the steam ferry. The cabin at space 61 is not a cheerful sight – some passengers appear seasick – though all arrive safely. By space 64, the traveler is himself ill and must take some restorative medicine. At space 68, he transfers to the post-carriage and, after some trouble with customs at the frontier, arrives at his destination. This game, then, tells a simple story of travel adventures overcome.

Steamboat Game. Arnhem: De Jong

about 1835

The *Steamboat Game* is a two-dice race game with its theme the steam ferry plying between Amsterdam and Zaandam, just across the river – these days a five-minute rail journey. The boat illustrated is the Mercurius, which was built in 1824 and began to ply the Amsterdam-Zaandam route in 1826. The game probably dates from the following decade. The goal at the end of the irregular 60-space track is the Czaar Peterhuisje, Peter the Great's historic house in Zaandam. The on-board amenities of the first-, second- and third-class cabins are contrasted at spaces 7, 9 and 11. A separate rule-sheet gives the tariff for these spaces as 5, 3 and 2 cents respectively. Further payments are due for a fresh pipe of tobacco, a glass of *Jenever* [Hollands gin] and a cup of coffee. On the way, you may have to pay at the Willemsluis [the William I lock that forms the connection with the North Holland Canal]. If you land at Zaandam, you are out of the game. Going further, you may need a horse carriage and a porter to take you and your luggage onwards and if you stay at the inn there will be more to pay. Though this print is just a cheap woodcut, it is attractive in its direct simplicity.

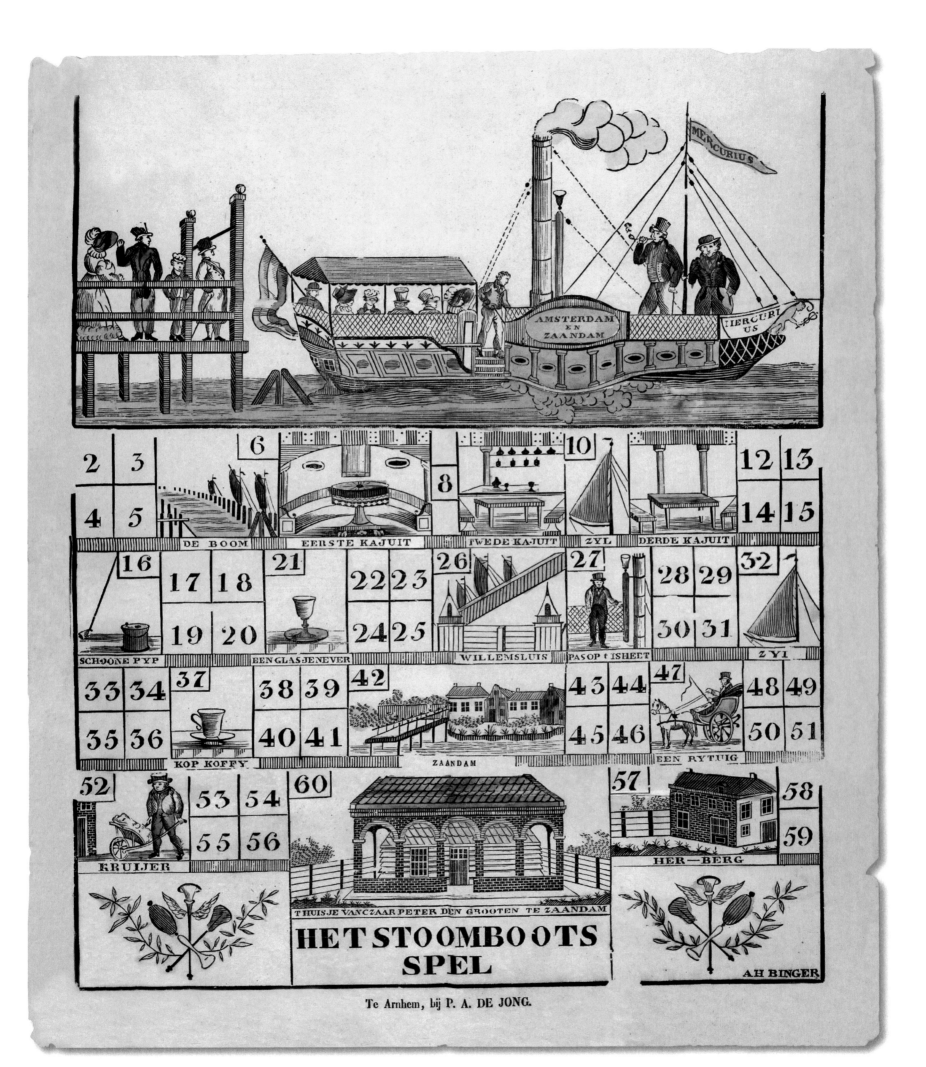

DE BOOM — EERSTE KAJUIT — TWEDE KAJUIT — ZYL — DERDE KAJUIT

SCHOONE PYP — EEN GLAS JENEVER — WILLEMSLUIS — PAS OP t IS HEET — ZYl

KOP KOFFY — ZAANDAM — EEN RYTUIG

KRUIJER — T HUISJE VAN CZAAR PETER DEN GROOTEN TE ZAANDAM — HER — BERG

HET STOOMBOOTS SPEL

A.H. BINGER

Te Arnhem, bij P. A. DE JONG.

NEDERLANDSCHE RIJNSPOORWEG-GEZELSCHAPSSPEL.

Gedeponeerd.

's HAGE.

Voorburg 31
30
Soetermeer Segwaard 29
Zevenhuizen
Wachter 28
Rotterdam 27
26
Capelle 25
Nieuwerkerk
Moordrecht 24

Sein Klok 33
Wachter 34
53 Zandwagen
Emmerich 52
Ellen 51
Wachter

de Bilt 35
Wagon 3e Klasse 36
Goederenwagen
Beestenwagen
Utrecht

36

Amsterdam

37 Driebergen
Wagon 3e Klasse 57
Wagon 3e Klasse

Maarsbergen 38
Wagon 2e Klasse 58
Wagon 1e Klasse 59
Kon. Ned. Brievenpost. 60
Conducteur Wagon 61
Kolenwagen 62

Veenendaal 39
Ede 40
Wolfhezen 41
Arnhem 42
Wachter
Velp 44
Westervoort 45

AMSTERDAM.

1
Sein Paal 2
Abcoude 3
Vreeland 4
Wachter 5
Nieuwersluis 6
Breukelen 7
Sein Klok 8
Maarsen 9

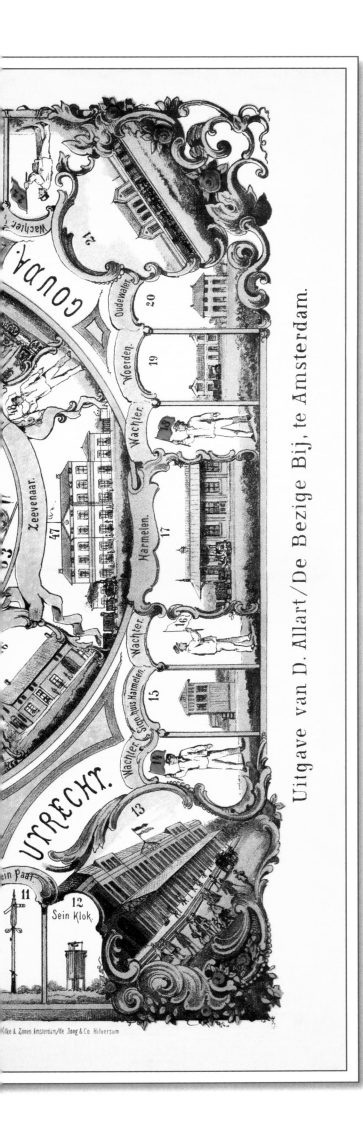

Uitgave van D. Allart/De Bezige Bij, te Amsterdam.

Rhine Railway Game. Amsterdam: Allart

about 1870

The *Rhine Railway Game* is also based on a real transport system. It celebrates the Nederlandsche Rijnspoorweg-Maatschappij (NRS). The company built a line from Amsterdam to Utrecht, opening in 1843, then to Arnhem, and finally in 1856 on to Germany. The game itself was published in 1874. Its track length of 63 spaces is the same as that of the Game of the Goose but the detailed rules are different. The depiction of the train, shown along the latter part of the track, is particularly attractive, with the conductor's carriage and the post-carriage following the locomotive and tender, then first-, second- and several third-class carriages, and finally the goods, cattle and open wagons. The depictions of the many stations along the route are interesting in their individuality and indeed form a useful historic record. This game is a chromolithograph, its bright, appealing colors being achieved at relatively low cost compared with hand coloring.

Game of the Traveler in Europe.
Paris: Basset
1830

In the *Game of the Traveler in Europe*, the places of interest are the famous sights of Europe. It is a 63-space game closely modeled on the Game of the Goose. The spaces along the track are filled with finely detailed representations of Europe's major buildings. The favorable Goose-type spaces, where the throw is doubled, show cathedrals and other important churches. The *bridge* space at number 6 shows the famous Westminster Bridge in London. Other classic hazards are treated appropriately. Thus the *death* space shows the tomb of the Queen of Denmark, while the *well* space shows the aqueduct in Seville, Spain, and the *prison* space shows the impressive fortress constructed by Vauban at Lille. The original edition of this game was published in the imperial era of Napoleon I. When he abdicated and the Bourbons were restored, political correctness demanded that the word 'imperial' in the text of the game should be replaced by 'royal'. This was done by altering the printing plate rather than going to the expense of having a new one engraved. Careful inspection of the text reveals small gaps where this has been done.

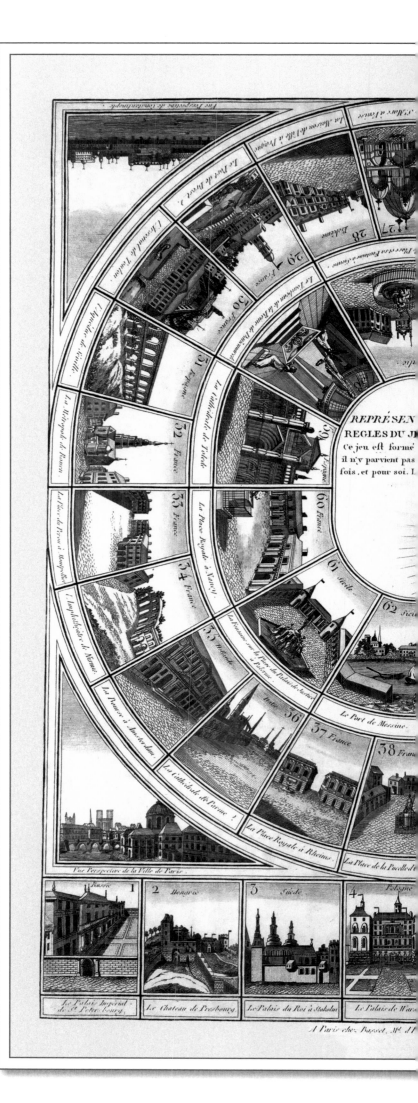

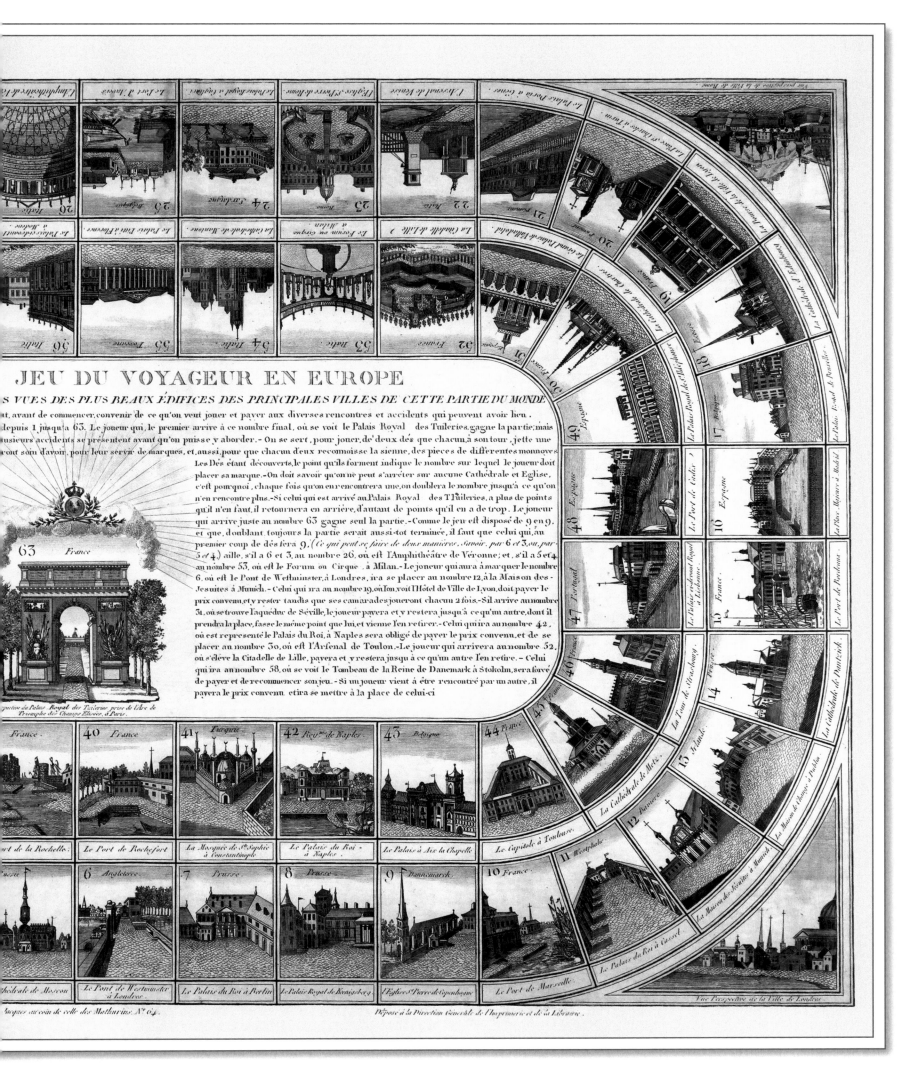

L'Orient, or the Indian Travelers.
London: Ogilvy
1846

L' *Orient, or the Indian Travelers* is one of the most splendid
of the games produced in London in the mid-nineteenth century.
The drawing is of high standard (probably by a known artist,
J W Barfoot, R.A.) and the hand coloring meticulous – this was
an up-market game. It is in fact two games in one. The scenes
surrounding the central map on its left, right and lower sides
show events in the history of India, very much from an English
viewpoint. Each player chooses one of the English Sovereigns
shown above the map. The players then in turn draw from
a bag cards naming one of the events. The player must then
name the Sovereign in whose reign the event occurred and, if
correct, may place the card on the picture of the event.
There are six events in each reign and play goes on until all six
in one of the reigns are covered, when the player representing
that Sovereign wins the game.

The second game is a race along one of the three routes
indicated on the map: overland via Marseilles (red); overland via
Trieste (yellow); or by sea, round the Cape of Good Hope. Play
is controlled by a teetotum with colored sides that advances the
player on the route whose color is turned up. The rules say that
'persons *residing* in India may make the starting point Calcutta
instead of London' – this is a game of the British Colonial era at
its height.

ORIENT
OR THE
INDIAN TRAVELLERS

HISTORICAL GAME

Round the World in Eighty Days. Paris: JJF

about 1906

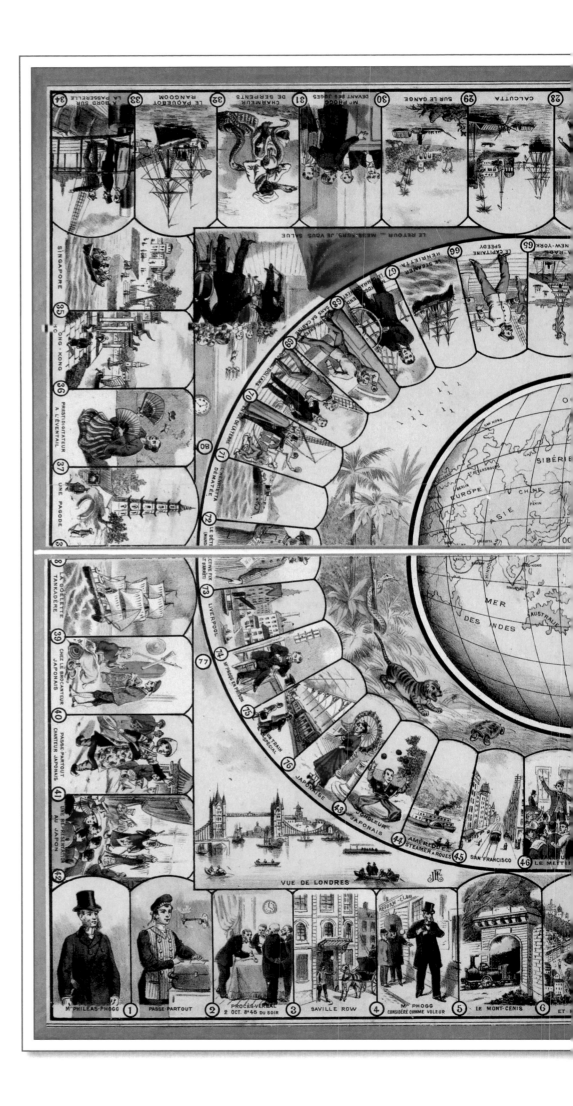

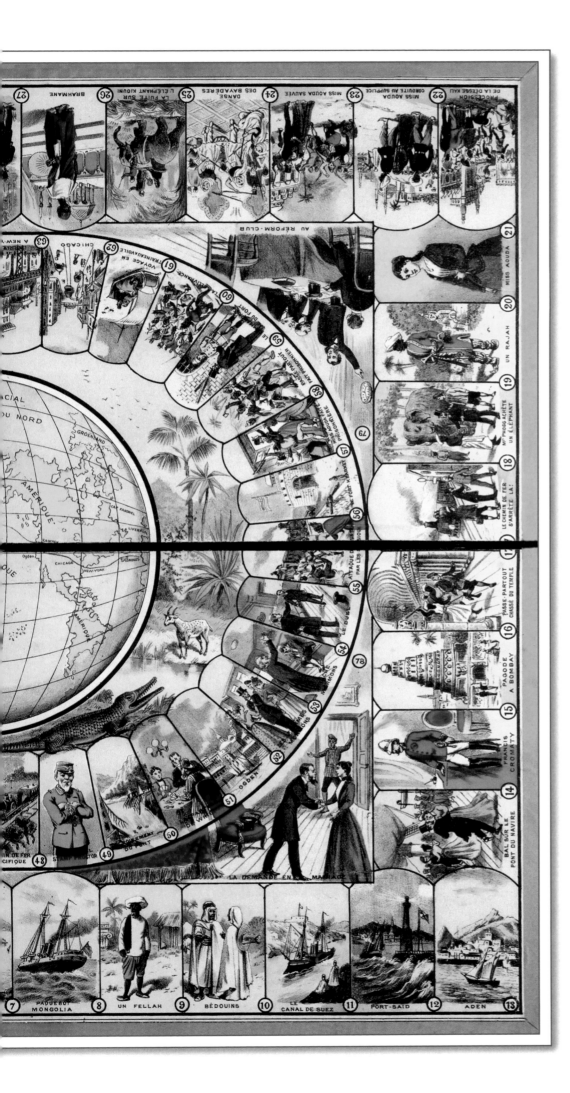

Jules Verne's novel of adventure, *Round the World in Eighty Days*, appeared in France in 1873. In the story, Phileas Fogg, a London Gentleman, attempts to go round the World with his French valet, Passe-partout, for a bet of £20,000. The story was hugely popular and several board games based on the story were soon published. The game shown here, a most beautiful chromolithograph, appeared a little later, in 1906. The 80-space track – one for each day, of course – surrounds the central map of the World, which shows the path taken by the travelers. The last four spaces are in the angles between the outer and inner sections of the track. Of the many adventures depicted, one of the most dramatic occurs at space 59, where the traveler is taken prisoner by the Redskins and must wait for another to come and help – as in the 'prison' rule for the Goose game.

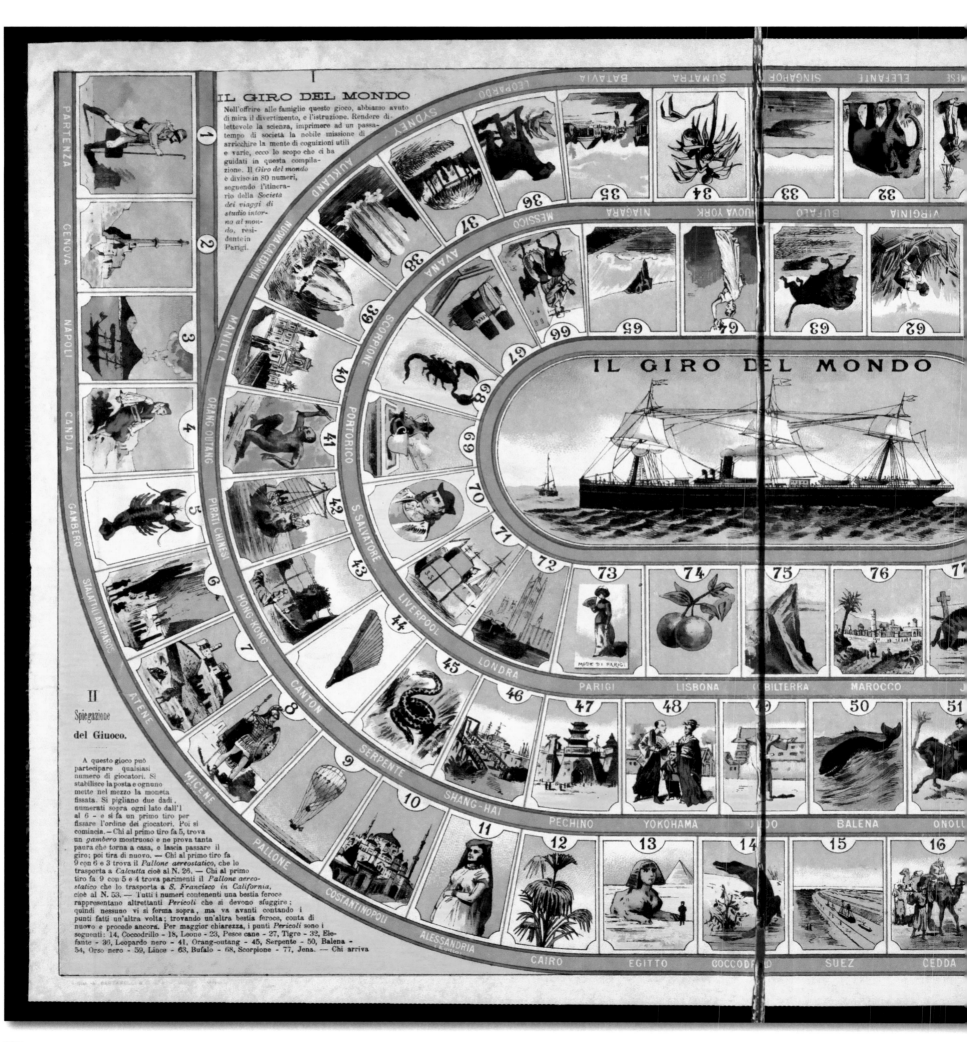

III

a *Suez*, cioè al N. 15, deve pagare il diritto di passaggio alla Compagnia del Canale e va direttamente in *Aden*, cioè al N. 20. — Chi va al N. 21, entra in *Quarantena*, e sta un giro senza giocare. — Chi va al N. 31, trova i *Questurini* del Regno di Siam che si insospettiscono di lui, e lo mettano in prigione. Deve quindi stare colà finchè sia cavato da un altro, con cui cambia il posto. Se nessuno arriva, dopo un giro, paga ancora la posta e tira innanzi. — Chi va al N. 42 trova i *Pirati Chinesi*, e per non esser preso, scappa indietro sino a *Sydney* in Australia, cioè al N. 37, pagando il convenuto. — Chi va al N. 52 trova una *Burrasca* terribile che lo rimanda a *Bombay* nelle Indie Inglesi, cioè al N. 22. — Chi va al N. 71 deve pagare il dazio a *Liverpool*, per la

IV

sua entrata in Inghilterra. — Chi al N. 56 cade in potere degli Indiani *Pelli-Rosse* che lo mangiano vivo. E finita per lui, e non gioca più. — Chi passa il N. 80 torna indietro contando i punti fatti in più; se incontra una bestia feroce, indietreggia ancora, ricontando i punti. — Chi va ad un numero in cui v'è già un altro, cambia con questi il posto. — Qualora avvenisse, cosa però non molto probabile, che tutti i giocatori cadessero in mano degli Indiani *Pelli Rosse*, al N. 58, e fossero mangiati vivi, si rimette un altra posta e si ricomincia il gioco.

Tour of the World.
Milan: Bertarelli

about 1890

With its 80-space track, Bertarelli's *Tour of the World* game was clearly stimulated by Verne's novel. In contrast, however, this game represents a real tour, not an imagined one. The text at the upper left of the game sheet explains that the game is based on an itinerary suggested by the Society for Study Tours around the World [SVEAM], a travel agency based in Paris and founded in 1878. The Goose spaces are occupied by dangerous animals, from which the traveler must flee at once, by the usual throw-doubling rule. More realistically, the Suez Canal (space 15) conveys the travelers directly to Aden. The game shares with the Jules Verne game above the difficulties with Redskins, though here (space 56) the unfortunate traveler is eaten alive and takes no further part in the game.

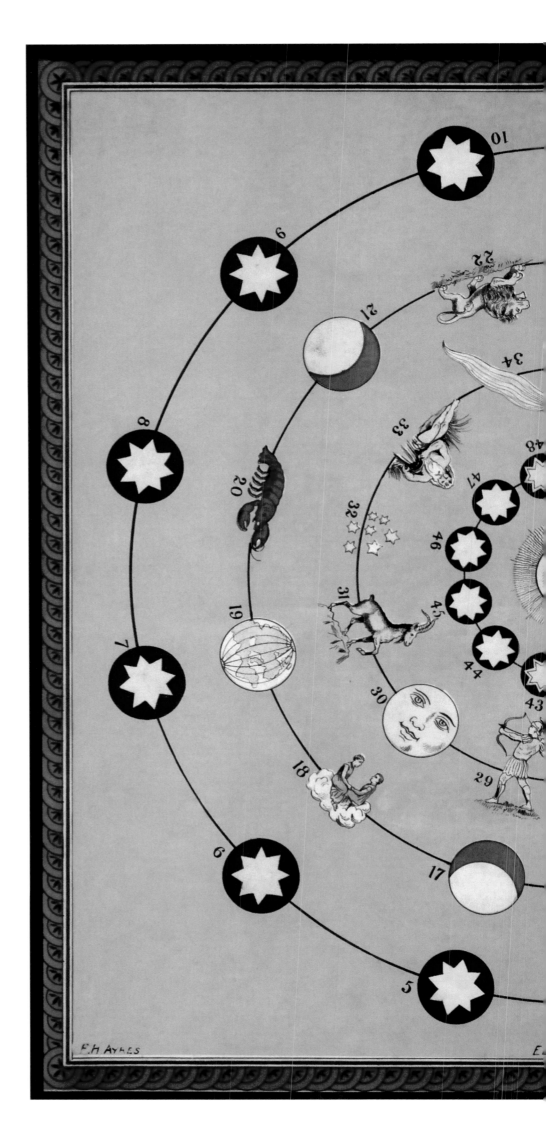

Aphelion. London: Ayres

about 1890

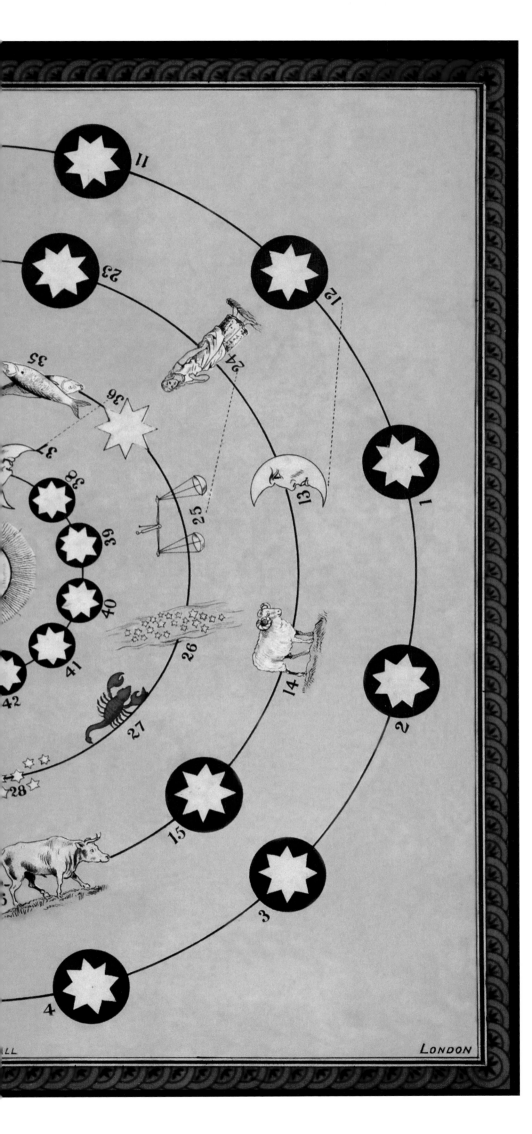

The game of *Aphelion* [to the Sun] is a single-dice game representing a wholly imaginary voyage from the stars to the Sun. Its numbered track of 50 spaces occupies four concentric circles, the outermost containing the fixed stars, the next two the zodiacal signs and the innermost containing the planets. An oddity is that (according to the rule leaflet): 'the Earth and Moon have been placed in the zodiac circles to give more amusement and sport'. The leaflet also claims that the game: 'will engrave in the memory an everlasting idea of the Solar and Planetary system' – one hopes that such a strange idea of astronomy as the game presents will in fact fade before too long! After such high claims, the game itself is rather dull, with (mostly) a succession of simple rules to pay or take from the pool. However, if a lady lands at space 24 (The Virgin), she is to receive a counter from each gentleman present, as well as five from the pool.

Games of War, Siege and Joust: Contests of the Imagination

Games to encourage interest in the army or navy also featured games of skill, for example where a fortress was besieged. In the beautiful German Game of the Knights, the player had to overcome many fairy-tale perils to become worthy of the final joust.

Educational games whose themes were the Arts of War were first developed in France at the end of the seventeenth century, when this subject was part of the curriculum that every boy of aristocratic descent would be expected to learn. The art of fortification was important in those days, and boys in France studied the design of castles according to principles laid down by the Marquis de Vauban (1633-1707), a famous French engineer. Games featuring the Navy were not neglected and boys would not only learn about the dangers of the sea while playing them, but would also be presented with a useful vocabulary of terms used in describing ships of war. These games of wooden sailing ships were popular and continued well into the nineteenth century (see The New Game of the Imperial Navy*). The French original of this game was plagiarized abroad – for example, an English version,* The Bulwark of Britannia*, appeared in 1797. It was exactly the same game, but was re-drawn to suit the British market, with a central scene of a 'Sea Fight' showing: 'The glorious victory obtained by Admiral Duncan over the Dutch fleet on the 11th of October 1797'.*

By the end of the nineteenth century, war on land had become much more technical than in the days of fortified castles and the earlier games had lost much of their relevance. The new games that came on to the market, though often still following the simple layout of the Game of the Goose, reflected this change in the treatment of their themes. Indeed, some of the games are valuable to the military historian for their careful depiction of the details of soldiering at that time, with innovations such as the use of bicycles for carrying dispatches.

National pride was at its most evident in these games, whatever their country of origin. The theme might be the glorious military history of that country, or simply pride in the regiment of the day. Several games took as their theme the progress of a young recruit through the ranks to fame and glory as Admiral or Field-Marshal. That such a positive outcome was only a rare consequence of joining up was something easily forgotten in playing these games and, though the games were not entirely silent about the perils of war, the 'bad spaces' were always in a minority. These games were probably not specifically designed to recruit boys and young men but their influence in promoting a military culture should not be ignored. Games which had as their theme the account of a particular campaign in which the country of origin was victorious must have contributed similarly to this culture.

Combat, though, could also have a softer side. The German Ritterspiel *[Game of the Knights]*, invented at the very end of the eighteenth century, was conceived as a romantic fairy-tale of trials to be surmounted by the aspiring knight. Only after success in these could the aspirant become a knight, to wait patiently until another player also came though the perils to become his opponent in the final combat to the death. A game only for boys, you might think? No, the rules provide for an occasion when one of the female players may bestow a chaste kiss!

Although most of the games in this chapter are of the familiar roll-and-move type, with movement along a track controlled solely by the throw of dice, an exception is the Game of Assault, which is a 'mind' game between two players, one of whom controls the two 'officers' defending a castle while the other controls the 'rebels' trying to overcome them. Games on this pattern have a long history, with the original versions pitting foxes against geese. This forms yet another example of how a game can be adapted to its time without the pattern of its play being changed.

The New Game

of the Imperial Navy.

Paris: Basset

about 1810

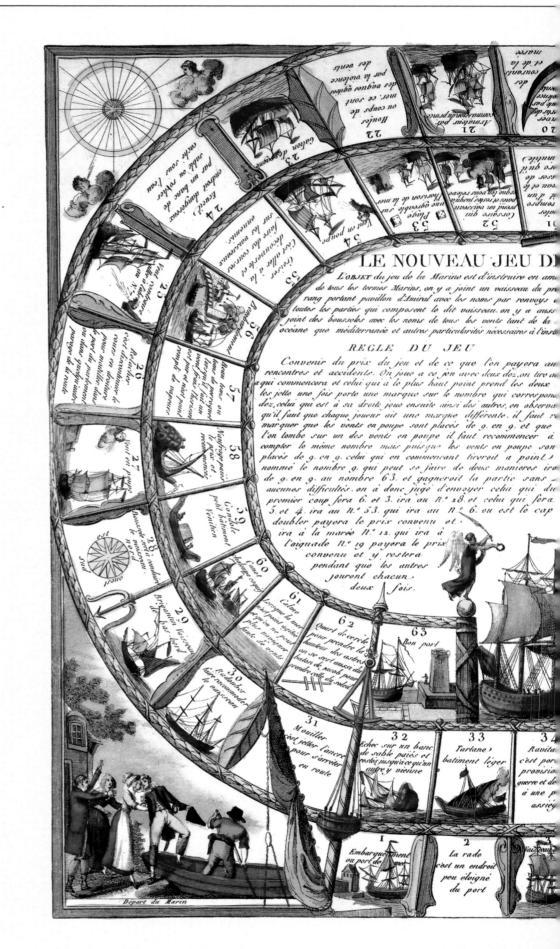

The *Game of the Imperial Navy* is one of the most attractive re-interpretations of the Game of the Goose. The 63-space spiral represents the voyage of a naval ship from embarkation to arrival at a safe harbor. The favorable spaces, on which the throw is doubled, represent 'wind on the poop', i.e. a favorable following wind. Another favorable space is number 6, a cape. Sailing round a cape was called 'doubling' the cape – and indeed here the point is doubled to space 12. But there are of course hazards along the way. At space 32, the vessel grounds on a shoal and must await assistance from another. At space 52, the vessel is taken prisoner by Corsairs [pirates] and again must await assistance, just as in the 'prison' rule of the parent game. The equivalent of the *death* space is at the expected space 58 and is a shipwreck, so that the player must start again. A good educational feature is that the inactive spaces contain short definitions of naval technical terms, often with an explanatory picture. Rather curiously, the long list of parts of a ship in the central space has no corresponding labeled image to which the list should properly refer – something left out when the game was updated to Napoleonic times.

Historical Game of the French Military.

Épinal: Pellerin

about 1860

This historical game tells the story of French military power across the ages. It is a 63-space game based on the Game of the Goose. Here, every ninth space is favorable, showing the Vendôme Column bedecked with flags. The column was erected by Napoleon I to celebrate his victory at Austerlitz in 1805 and was topped by his statue. Though the column would later be torn down by the Paris Commune of the 1870s, who saw it as a symbol of war and conquest, it was soon rebuilt. The object of the game is to reach the Arc de Triomphe. The track is decorated with many scenes of French triumphs, e.g. space 4 shows Clovis, first King of the Franks, succeeding in battle at Tolbiac, around 500 A.D. One of the hazard spaces (number 15) shows Joan of Arc taken prisoner, with the usual *prison* rule. Others show French defeats. For example, space 20 shows the French routed by the Italian forces at the battle of Pavia in 1525: the player landing there is *hors de combat* and must stay there for two turns 'in taking the wounded' to space 40, *Les Invalides* in Paris, the hospital for military veterans. Space 55 shows Waterloo (1815) with the *death* rule, 'start again'. The penultimate space brings us up to date, showing victory against Austria at the Battle of Solferino in 1859 for the French forces under Napoleon III and the Sardinian forces under Victor-Emmanuel II. This would have been a good game to play, perhaps also exciting a welcome curiosity about the events depicted.

Game of the Knights. Prague: Fraza

about 1820

This version of the romantic Game of the Knights, printed in Prague for the German market, has instructions written in each of the active spaces, most requiring the player to move forward or back as specified. It tells the story of a young man aspiring to knighthood as he journeys along the outer track. There are many hazards to overcome. To cross the water at space 11, you must throw doublets [both dice showing the same point]. Several wizards may be encountered, some helpful, others not so. At the inn (space 19) you must pay for lodging but may throw again. Winning your spurs at space 33 also merits another throw. The 'unhappy' space to beware of is at number 60, showing an unhorsed knight, where you must begin the game again. More happily, if you succeed in reaching space 61, you will be dubbed a knight and can enter the final contest – but before it can begin, you must wait for another player to win through to knighthood, to become your opponent. The two knights then battle it out along the central track of 24 small squares. Here, it is sudden death – if you land on a skull, your opponent wins. Other versions of the game have elaborate rule booklets. These make clear that the game was envisaged as being played by young people of both sexes, with sometimes the young knight winning a kiss from his damsel.

The Regiment.

Designed by Ludovic.

Paris: Mauclair-Dacier

about 1895

This fine chromolithograph shows the progress of a young recruit through the ranks of the French army: the meticulous depiction of uniforms is typical of the wonderful detail of this game. The scenes of army life go well beyond combat and parades. Thus, at the beginning of the track we see the drawing of lots to determine who will be called up and the ensuing medical examination – one recruit looks to have bow legs and may not pass – and the arrival at the regiment. The tedium of the soldier's day is not forgotten: at space 20, we see *l'astiquage* - spit-and-polish. Offending because of 'bad turn-out' is at space 22. Towards the end of the track, the most up-to-date technology is deployed: the dispatch-rider on his bicycle, the telegraphists (using wires rather than radio) and the military balloon for observation of artillery fire. This, though, is a very human portrayal of military life – see the Reservist at space 52 saying goodbye to his wife and their babe-in-arms, or the joy of coming home on a leave pass. But death on the field of honour strikes, on the traditional space 58, while the dishonor of being stripped of rank is shown at space 64. The goal is of course Victory, with a grateful populace welcoming the Regiment as liberators. This is a game to be savored visually.

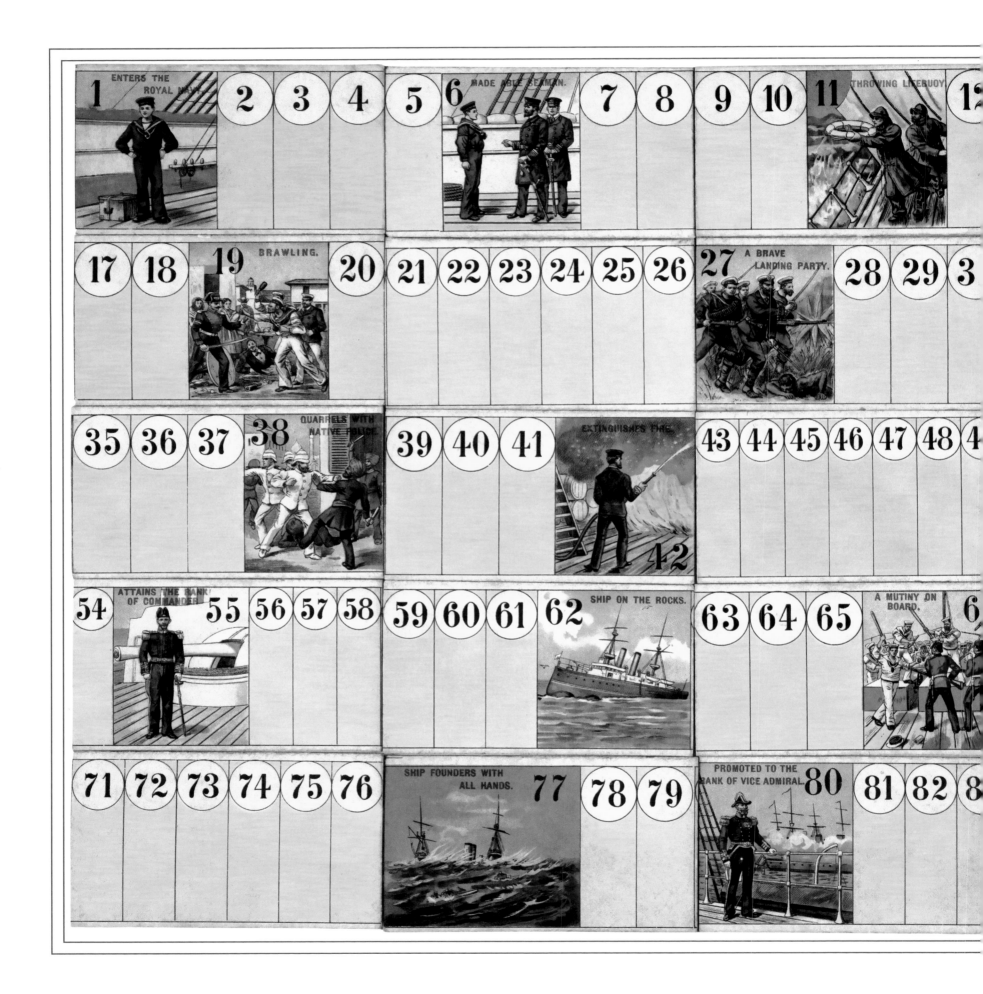

Here we have a board game without a board! Or, rather, the board comes as a pack of numbered cards, to be laid out to the player's preferred shape of track. A whole series of games on this pattern were produced by the London firm of C W Faulkner & Co. The first of these was called *Upidee* and was on the theme of a horse race, over fences. The game shown here represents a sailor-boy's ideal career in the Royal Navy, as he becomes first an Able Seaman, then Boatswain, before being promoted to Officer rank, successively as Commander, Captain and Vice-Admiral. On the way are all sorts of naval adventures, some less likely than others. Saving the Captain from sharks earns him a medal – and another turn. More credible is the Court-martial at space 50, where he is tried for drunkenness on duty and loses five years' seniority [promotion in the Royal Navy of that time depended on years served at a particular rank]. He must go back to space 39 and pay three counters into the pool. But a worse fate threatens at space 62 – his error of navigation causes his ship to hit the rocks. He is dismissed from the Service – and must retire from the game. This is an attractive game – the bright, chromolithographed sailor-boys in their uniforms are instantly appealing.

Boer and Rooinek Game.

Designed by E G Schlette.

Amsterdam: Koster Bros.

about 1900

The *Boer and Rooinek Game* is indeed a crude production – but the caricatures have great impact. 'Rooinek' [from the Afrikaans, meaning 'Red-neck'] is a derogatory word, still used for an English-speaking South African. It is said to derive from the sunburnt necks of the British soldiers fighting in South Africa. The game was published during the Second Boer War fought between the British Empire and two Boer states, the South African Republic and the Orange Free State, from 1899 to 1902. At first, the Boers were largely victorious. They won significant battles at Colenso, Magersfontein and Stormberg, also laying siege to Ladysmith, Kimberley, and Mafeking [now Mahikeng]. The game reflects these early successes, as evident from the pained expression on the face of the British soldier and the glee on the face of the Boer. Later in the war, however, the British brought in overwhelming forces, so that the outcome was never in doubt. The game has two opposing numbered tracks. The Boers start at Pretoria and follow the white track, heading for Kaapstad [Capetown] as their winning space, number 144. The Rednecks follow the yellow track, in the reverse direction. The red and blue tracks are short-cuts, to be followed by the Rednecks and by the Boers, respectively, whenever they come to a joining point on their tracks. The game has its own complicated rules.

New Game of Besieging.

Amsterdam: [probably] Vlieger

about 1880

This is an unusual presentation in which an earlier game sheet is reproduced in the upper left corner of a larger sheet, on which the rules have been added, together with lively scenes of combat as decoration. The earlier sheet dates from about 1860, as determined from the central picture. The main figure has been recognized as a likeness of King William III, who was King of the Netherlands and Grand Duke of Luxembourg from 1849 until his death in 1890. He is pictured as the commander-in-chief of the army, in the uniform of the Royal Netherlands Army for the period 1854-1865. The game is played with double dice on the 56-space track. The players throw for the start, and the player with the highest throw becomes the General. On the way to the battlefield, there are many hazards, as shown by the small pictures. For all of these there are detailed rules. For example, at space 11, which shows the King, you must pay ten counters to buy a good place to watch him go by. In the cell at space 14, you must stay overnight and let your turn pass, as also at space 28, which shows sentry duty. At space 52, you are recognized as a spy dressed as an organ-grinder: you are shot in front of the troops and (as for the death space in the Goose game) must begin the game again.

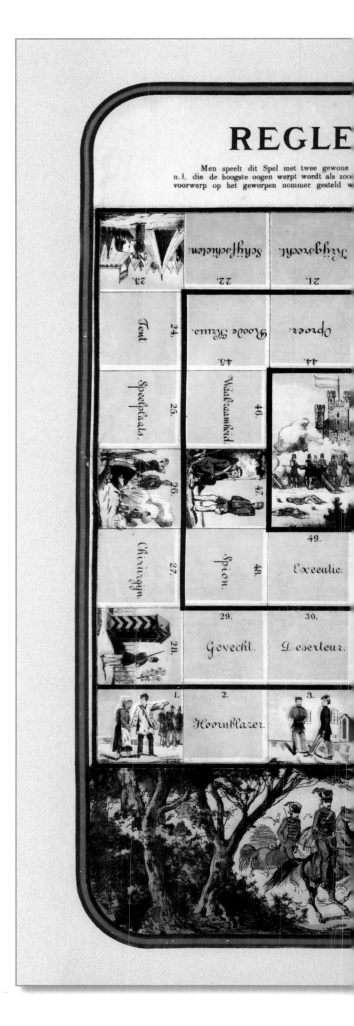

NIEUW BELEGERINGSPEL.

Als inleg wordt door elk der medespelenden een overeen te komen getal fishes of penningen in den pot gedaan. Vervolgens wordt overgegaan tot het benoemen van een Generaal, hetgeen door het lot wordt beslist. Hij ... d en kiest zich als zijnen adjudant-betaalmeester, den oudste in jaren van het gezelschap. De Generaal speelt het eerst en heeft het recht de door hem geworpen oogen te doen gelden of wel op nieuw te gooien. Een klein ... or hij is. Hij geeft vervolgens de dobbelsteenen aan zijn rechterbuur, en zoo doet elk op zijnen beurt, tot dat een der manschappen eindelijk het slagveld (No. 56) bereikt, en het spel wint. Op den weg echter naar het slagveld ontmoet men tal van hindernissen, waarvoor de volgende regels gelden: Wie op 3 komt en verzuimt voor den hem passeerenden kapitein te salueeren betaalt *zes* penningen, en wie op 6 komt *vier* penningen tot onderhoud van den trommel, doch heeft daarvoor het recht direct tot 12 door te marcheeren. Wie op 8 komt blaast op de trompet en ontvangt daarvoor *drie* penningen, terwijl hij die op 11 komt zich voor *tien* penningen eene goede plaats koopt om den Koning te zien passeeren. Wie in de Cachot (14) komt, moet daar overnachten en dus zijn beurt ééns laten voorbijgaan. Wie op 16 komt ontvangt *zes* penningen en wie op 20 komt, wordt in de vesting opgesloten, ten zij hij *vier* penningen losgeld betale. Wie op 23 komt huurt eene veldtent voor den nacht, volgens tarief *tien* penningen. Wie op 26 komt gebruikt in het Bivouak zijn ontbijt, waarvoor hij 5 penningen verschuldigd is. Wie op 28 komt, lost den schildwacht af en blijft aldaar op zijn post tot hij op zijne beurt, verlost wordt. Op 31 gekomen neemt men van de marketenster een glaasje bier voor *drie* penningen. Wie op 34 komt ontvangt voor elke weg te dragen korf van iederen speler *een* penning, ze moeten echter naar het slagveld gebracht worden, hetgeen veel tijd kost. Hierdoor heeft hij geen tijd verder te gaan en laat zijn beurt *drie* maal passeeren. Wie op 36 komt betaald voor den aankoop van **kruit** *tien* penningen en wie op 39 komt vraagt den weg naar No. 47 om zijn wonden te laten verbinden. Hij betaalt daarvoor *vier* penningen aan zijnen linker- en rechter nevenman, doch vertrekt dan ook onmiddelijk derwaarts. Wie op 43 komt gaat onmiddelijk terug naar den Koning (No. 11) om hem mede te deelen. dat de Vesting in brand staat, hij ontvangt 12 penningen reisgeld. Wie op 47 komt betaald tot instandhouding van het fonds: *het Roode Kruis* 8 penningen, doch zijn die van No. 39 derwaarts zijn gewezen hiervan uitgezonderd. Wie op 52 komt, wordt als Spion herkend in het gewaad van een orgeldraaier, om voor het front der troepen te worden gefusileerd. Hij begint daarop weder van voren aan. Wie op 56 komt wint het spel en wordt voor het volgende Generaal. Komt men *over* 56 dan worden zooveel punten achteruit geteld; tenzij men is overeengekomen, dat dan weder van voren af moet worden geworpen en de te veel geworpen punten van No. 1 af bijgeteld. Wie in dit geval op No. 1 komt ontvangt van elk *vijf* penningen reisgeld. Achterhalen twee spelers elkaar, dan neemt de eerst op de plaats vertoevende, de plaats in, waarvan de andere gekomen is; hij ontvangt daarvoor echter van dezen *twee* penningen.

Uitgave van VAN HOLKEMA & WARENDORF te Amsterdam

PREMIE op WARENDORF'S GEÏLLUSTREERDE FAMILIEKALENDE

Game of the Netherlands-Indies War.
Amsterdam: Warendorf
1903

This splendid large game-sheet was issued as a free appendix to Warendorf's *Illustrated Family Calendar* in 1903. The Calendar was an annual, offering 'nine fascinating novels' and sixteen color plates. The game sheet probably represents the Aceh War (1873-1914) in the Dutch East Indies. This was a colonial war that the Kingdom of the Netherlands waged with the aim of securing the Strait of Malacca, an important shipping lane between the Malay Peninsula and the Indonesian island of Sumatra, against pirates from Aceh, at the northern end of the island. The rules are simple. The track is indicated by numbered circles. At any red number, you pay so many stakes to the winner's pot as are indicated, whereas at a blue number you take so many. At a number marked with 'H', you go to the hospital at space 35 and pay to its separate pot, whereas at a number marked with 'A' you must go to the *ambulance* [field-hospital] at space 81. The winner receives a medal (the 'Knights Cross') and the contents of the pot, while the last patient in the hospital receives the hospital pot. A curious point is that the game illustration is re-drawn from an earlier game, published in 1879, with the addition of various palm trees and a building with an oriental dome. The earlier game represented a scene in the Boer War with no connection with the Far East. This may account for the sympathetic depiction of the Aceh warriors, who appear to be well organized in good defensive positions.

Hospitaal en wacht zoolang tot een ander hem aflost. — Die het Hospitaal verlaat begint van af Nº. 35 en betaalt één fiche aan de kas van het Hospitaal. — Die op een nummer komt, met A gemerkt, gaat terug naar Nº. 81 de Ambulance. — Die het eerst op Nº. 99 of daarboven komt is Winner van het Spel, ontvangt het Ridderkruis en den inhoud van den pot; terwijl alsdan de laatst verpleegde in het Hospitaal die kas ontvangt. Op Nº. 35 en 81 mogen zich meer dan een speler te gelijk bevinden.

AMST. BOEK- EN STEENDRUKKERIJ, v/h. ELLERMAN, HARMS & Co., Amsterdam.

Asalto. Barcelona: Paluzie

about 1900

*A*salto [meaning Assault] is a two-player game of skill and strategy known under many names. This version of the game is also known as *German Tactics*. To play this on the game sheet, you will need two counters of one color, to represent the Officers, and twenty-four of another color, to represent the Rebels. The two Officers, who defend the fortress at the top of the game sheet, start anywhere on the points numbered 1 to 9. The Rebels start on the 24 red points below the fortress. One player controls the Officers, the other the Rebels, each moving one counter in turn, with the Rebels moving first. The Rebels can move only forwards, to any adjacent unoccupied point along on any of the white lines; they cannot move along the black lines. The two Officers can move in any direction along any line to any adjacent unoccupied point. The Officers can also 'capture' [i.e. remove] a Rebel just as in Draughts, by jumping in any direction over him, provided that the landing point immediately beyond him is unoccupied. The jump must be in a straight line. The Officers themselves can never be captured, nor may they jump over one another. The Rebels win if they can drive both Officers out of the fortress and occupy all nine of the numbered points. The Officers win if they can reduce the number of Rebels so that this is not possible. Enjoy the struggle!

JUEGO DEL ASALTO

Este juego está dividido en cinco partes.—La parte superior, donde los puntos son numerados, representa la fortaleza que, defendida por 2 soldados solamente, ha de luchar contra las cuatro partes inferiores ocupadas por los sitiadores.—Los 2 soldados sitiados se colocan á voluntad sobre los puntos numerados y los soldados sitiadores se deben colocar sobre los 24 puntos rojos.—Los 24 soldados sitiadores sólo pueden avanzar por las líneas blancas en dirección recta ó diagonal, sin poder retroceder ni seguir las líneas negras.—A cada jugada uno de los soldados adelanta un paso del punto donde está al inmediato si está desocupado.—Los 2 soldados sitiados pueden seguir las líneas blancas ó negras y diagonales lo mismo avanzando que retrocediendo, y pueden situarse en todos los puntos que no sean ocupados.—Estos soldados á cada jugada adelantan un paso, excepto cuando toman un sitiador, lo cual se hace lo mismo que en el juego de Damas, es decir, que se puede tomar cada soldado sitiador detrás del cual se encuentre un punto desocupado; así mismo se pueden tomar varias, avanzando y retrocediendo.—Los 2 soldados sitiados deben procurar siempre poderse retirar á la fortaleza.—Los 24 sitiadores no pueden tomar ninguno de los sitiados; pero si les pueden soplar como en el juego de Damas cuando se descuidan de tomar á uno cualquiera de ellos.—La combinación de este juego consiste en expulsar los 2 defensores fuera de la fortaleza y ocupar los 9 puntos de ella con sitiadores.—Se juega por dos personas alternativamente como en el juego de Damas.—Para peones pueden utilizarse soldados de papel encartonados, recortados y con un pié de madera.

Imprenta Elzeviriana y Librería Camí, S. A., Calle Joaquín Costa, 64 - Barcelona

Sports and Leisure: Enjoy the Fun!

The printed race game is so adaptable that almost any activity can inspire a game: skating, cycling, tobogganing and fairground rides are examples. These games give vivid accounts of the culture of leisure in the nineteenth century.

In the later years of the nineteenth century, the earlier emphasis on games for the education of children and teenagers was supplanted by a wider range of games, with themes more representative of the leisure interests of adults. Some of these endeavored to reproduce the thrills of upper-class diversions, such as the horse races across country known as the steeplechase. These games often had as their main excitement the opportunity for gambling, just as in the real events. However, the middle classes in particular, benefiting from increased prosperity following industrial mechanization, found that time and money were available also for them to pursue non-utilitarian activities and diversions of all kinds. Manufacturers of games were quick to spot opportunities to satisfy each latest craze. Even though the games could

not possibly provide the direct enjoyment of the real thing, they often were surprisingly faithful to its characteristic excitements, displaying considerable inventiveness in doing so. For example, the cycling craze of the final decade of the century gave rise to games on this theme in many countries, all enlivened by the various different accidents that could befall the rider in those early days. It was a time of rapid development of cycling equipment and the designers of board games had to work quickly to keep up.

Another late-nineteenth-century craze was the sport of roller skating, which gave rise to an invented word, rinkomania to describe the unbridled enthusiasm of its devotees. Improvements in the design of the skate meant that the diversion became extremely popular in Europe towards the end of the nineteenth century, notwithstanding the kind of accidents and embarrassments shown in The Skating Rink, *a lively game illustrated at the beginning of this book, played by two teams on the two tracks. If the two teams come together where the tracks cross, they 'come* to grief and fall' and both must start the game afresh. But the real delight of the game lies in the details of the social scene – the variety of accidents and the reactions to them, the different costumes worn by personalities of all ages and classes as they mix together. From the outset, roller skating was a diversion where young people of both sexes could meet and enjoy some freedom from stultifying convention – a small but significant part of the sexual revolution.

To diversions of a sporting kind were added mechanized fairground attractions, some designed for young children, but others, such as the Great Wheel of the Paris Expo of 1900, were for a wider age range. These, too, found their expression in newly designed board games. The beautiful Game of the Flower Parade, is another example of how social activities were picked up as themes for games, the game sheet also serving to keep in memory a splendid royal event. In contrast, the Saint Nicholas Game sets its scene firmly within the Dutch household, on the night when present-giving and feasting is still the tradition in the Netherlands. Its attractive illustrations surely convey the children's sense of wonder on such a night.

Invention was at work in the adaptation of a different kind of game to the leisure market. This was the game of Snakes and Ladders – 'new' to Europe in the late nineteenth century, certainly, but based on a much older game of moral instruction, known in India, Nepal and Tibet perhaps as early as the thirteenth century. In the original versions, a player advanced up the board towards Vishnu or Nirvana, sometimes landing on spaces with virtues, which accelerated upward progress, or spaces labeled with vices, which led downwards along snakes. A simplified version of this game appeared in England in 1892, where it became a firm favorite with children. In continental Europe, where the basic Snakes and Ladders game itself never took hold, it nevertheless gave rise to thematic variations, including versions based on the circus and, in the game shown here, tobogganing on the ice.

The Steeplechase Game. Paris: Rousseau

about 1880

The Steeplechase Game represents a horse race over hedges, fences and ditches. The folding board is large, opening to 73 x 48 cm, and is lithographed in color, with further coloring by hand of the details. This game would have come with a handsome box of model horses, cast in metal and hand-painted, together with a set of fences and other obstacles to be placed on the track as decoration. The game was made in Paris for the English market and is of high quality – but inspection of the rules written in the center of the game reveals several mistakes in the English. This game was played for stakes. Players could take more than one horse but had to pay one-and-a-half stakes for every horse beyond the first. Space 57 shows a horse falling at a fence – the horse landing here must start again, without further penalty. But space 84, the water jump, is worse – a horse landing here must re-start and also a new stake must be paid. Spaces with their numbers in a circle act like stops, so that the horse must go back, and a similar rule applies to the hedges, barriers and ditches. The game is played with double dice except that the players may make it a shorter game by playing with four dice until near the end. One can imagine money changing hands at a great rate. Evidently the makers of the game were not confident that their rules were perfect. At the end, they say that the players: 'can themselves establish their own rules'.

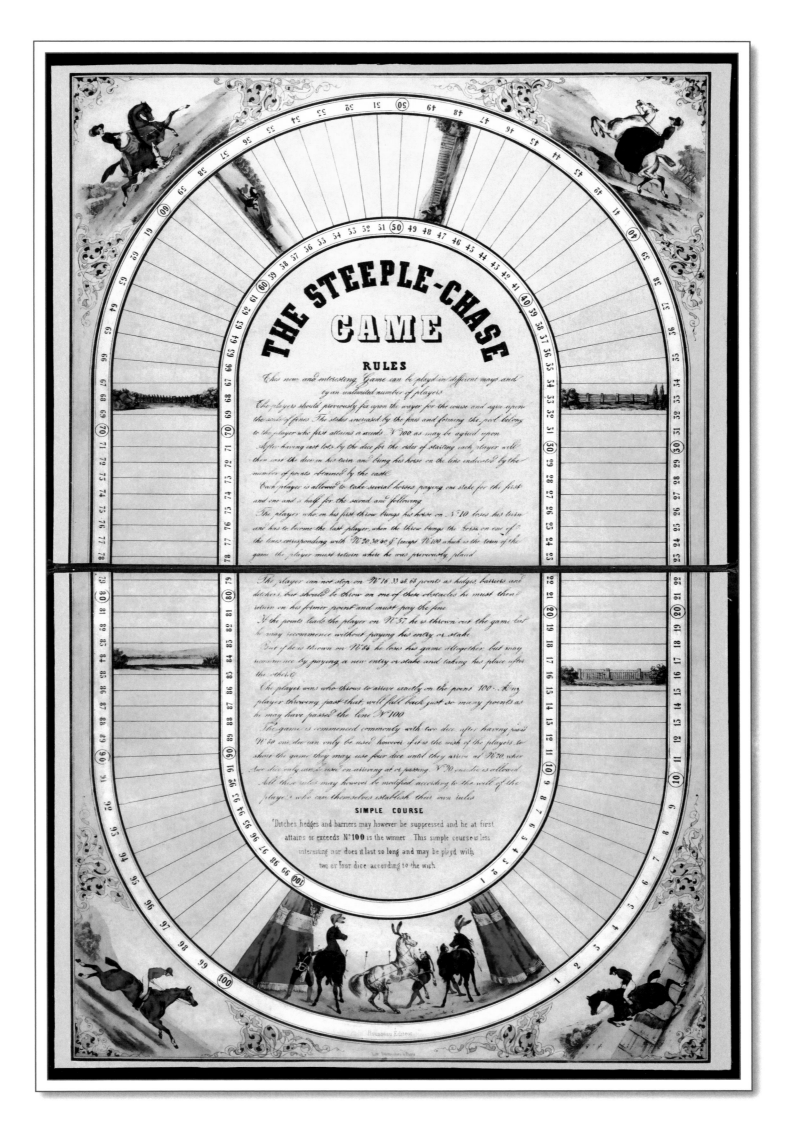

THE STEEPLE-CHASE GAME

RULES

This new and interesting Game can be played in different ways and by an unlimited number of players

The players should previously fix upon the wager for the course and agree upon the scale of fines. The stake increased by the fines and forming the pool belongs to the player who first attains or exceeds N° 100 as may be agreed upon

After having cast lots by the dice for the order of starting each player will then cast the dice in his turn and bring his horse on the line indicated by the number of points obtained by the cast

Each player is allowed to take several horses paying one stake for the first and one and a half for the second and following

The player who on his first throw brings his horse on N° 10 loses his turn and has to become the last player, when the throw brings the horse on one of the lines corresponding with N° 20, 30, 40 &° (except N° 100 which is the term of the game the player must return where he was previously placed

The player can not stop on N° 16, 33, 48, 68 points as hedges, barriers and ditches, but should he throw on one of these obstacles he must then return on his former point and must pay the fine

If the points leads the player on N° 57 he is thrown out the game but he may recommence without paying his entry or stake

But if he is thrown on N° 84 he loses his game altogether but may recommence by paying a new entry or stake and taking his place after the others

The player wins who throws to arrive exactly on the point 100. Any player throwing past that will fall back just so many points as he may have passed the line N° 100

The game is commenced commonly with two dice, after having passed N° 50 one die can only be used however if it is the wish of the players to shorten the game they may use four dice until they arrive at N° 70 when two dice only can be used on arriving at or passing N° 90 one die is allowed

All these rules may however be modified according to the will of the players who can themselves establish their own rules

SIMPLE COURSE

Ditches hedges and barriers may however be suppressed and he at first attains or exceeds N° 100 is the winner. This simple course is less interesting nor does it last so long and may be played with two or four dice according to the wish

Saint Nicholas Game. Amsterdam: Vlieger

about 1890

In the Netherlands, all good children welcome the visit of *Sinterklaas* or *Sint-Nicolaas*, a legendary figure based on Saint Nicholas, patron saint of children. The saint's name-day, on 6 December, is celebrated annually with the giving of gifts on St. Nicholas' Eve. *Sinterklaas* is the primary source of *Santa Claus* – our Father Christmas. The central decoration shows the saint being assisted in his task of giving out presents by *Zwarte Piet* [Black Peter], traditionally a Moor from Spain. The game is a clever adaptation of the Goose game to illustrate the happy customs of the evening. One of these customs is that presents for the children are left in boots or shoes – and in the game the favorable spaces, on numbers 9, 18, 27 etc. are appropriately indicated. Hazard spaces are re-interpreted for children: thus, the *Inn* becomes the Toyshop, where you pay and miss a turn, while the *Death* space becomes the sack of Black Peter, into which a naughty child has fallen head first, to be taken away. The initial throw of nine has special rules, different for boys and for girls. The player may be betrothed to an attractive young lady/young man at spaces 25/26 or to a not-so-attractive old lady/old man at spaces 51/53, depending on the detail of the throw.

Reglement
VAN HET
SINT NICOLAAS SPEL

Vooraf bepaalt men den inzet en speelt dit spel met twee dobbelsteenen.

Wie de hoogste oogen werpt speelt het eerst.

Als een heer bij de eerste worp 6 en 3 gooit *mag* hij gaan tot 25, of eene dame tot 26.

Werpt een heer terstond 5 en 4 dan *moet* hij gaan tot 51 of eene dame tot 53 en laten hunne beurt eens voorbijgaan.

Al wie komt op:
eene gevulde klomp of schoen mag nog eens zooveel voortstellen.

Op 6 moet men 1 betalen, doch dubbel betalende gaat men tot 12.

» 13 betaalt 3 en laat zijne beurt eens voorbijgaan.
» 19 » 2 en laat zijne beurt eens voorbijgaan.
» 31 » 3, blijft zitten tot hij verlost wordt en gaat dan 3 terug.
» 36 » 1; doch mag nog 7 voortstellen.
» 42 » 2 en telt 3 terug.
» 52 » 3, moet wachten tot hij door een ander wordt vervangen en dan 3 terugstellen.
» 58 » 4 en moet van voren af aan beginnen.

Wie zonder 6 en 3 of 5 en 4 te werpen toch komt op 25, 26, 51 of 53 moet 1 betalen doch 3 voortstellen.

Wie door een ander wordt ingehaald betaalt 1 en gaat in diens plaats terug.

Wie over 63 komt telt terug, en komt men op een schoen dan moet men nog eens zooveel voortstellen als men geworpen heeft.

Wie op 62 komt wint de pot en speelt in het volgende spel weder eerst.

Lith. Gebr Brockensiek.

UITGAVE van J. VLIEGER, AMSTERDAM.

135

REGLEMENT

Dit spel kan door 2 of meer personen gespeeld worden. Ieder speler neemt een onderscheiden voorwerp om op te zetten. Men bepaalt een zeker getal fiches en deponeert dit als inzet in den pot (n°. 88). Wie (met 2 dobbelsteenen) de hoogste oogen werpt, begint het eerst.

Wie op n°. **3** komt, mag 2 plaatsen vooruitgaan omdat hij een versierde wagen tegen komt die naar het Corso-terrein gaat.

Wie op n°. **7** komt moet tol betalen: 1 fiche in den pot.

Wie op n°. **9** komt moet zijn beurt eens laten voorbijgaan wegens reparatie aan zijn fiets en betaalt 1 fiche in den pot.

Wie op n°. **17** komt moet van af 1 beginnen omdat hij niet voldaan heeft aan de voorgeschreven bepaling.

Wie op n°. **19** komt is bekroond, mag 3 plaatsen vooruitgaan en bekomt 1 fiche uit de pot.

Wie op n°. **23** komt blijft uitrusten totdat hij zijn plaats voor een ander moet inruimen en betaalt 1 fiche voor vertering in den pot.

Wie op n°. **25** komt heeft den tweeden prijs en mag zich tweemaal zooveel verplaatsen als hij oogen geworpen heeft.

Wie op n°. **49** komt moet 4 plaatsen terug en zijn beurt eens voorbij laten gaan omdat hij zoo roekeloos gereden heeft.

Wie op n°. **67** komt mag als ontwerper van den boog 2 plaatsen vooruit gaan en krijgt 1 fiche uit den pot.

Wie op n°. **71** komt rijdt op een verboden weg en moet terug naar **66**.

Wie op n°. **81** komt mag als belooning voor zijn moeite op **84** gaan staan.

Wie op n°. **88** komt ontvangt voor de beste inzending den **1sten** prijs en heeft den pot gewonnen.

Wie voorbij n°. **88** werpt moet even zooveel oogen terug tellen als hij te veel geworpen heeft.

Komt iemand juist achter een ander te staan, b. v. op **22** als 21 reeds is bezet, dan mag hij den laatste overspringen en komt daardoor op **22**, terwijl de andere zijn spel op nieuw moet beginnen en een fiche in den pot betaalt.

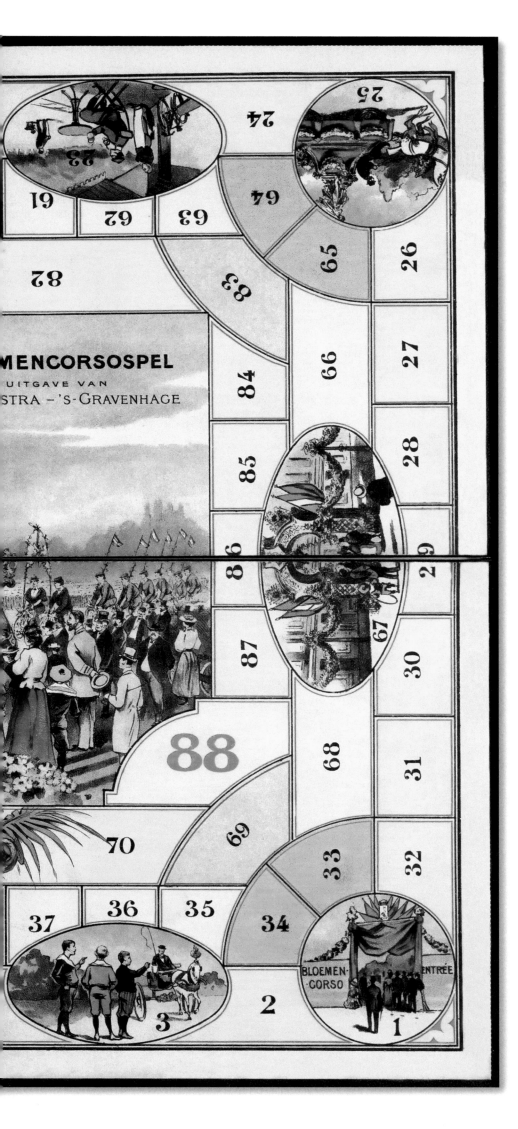

Flower parades are an integral part of Netherlands tradition, occurring in spring time throughout the bulb-growing region. The parade in The Hague that is pictured in this game celebrates a special event: the inauguration of Queen Wilhelmina. She was born in 1880 and became Queen of the Netherlands on the death of King William III in 1890, though her mother acted as regent until 1898, when Wilhelmina was old enough to be sworn in. The game shows her watching the parade from a curtained dais, with her mother and other members of the royal family. The float drawn by four horses and decorated in the royal color orange, surmounted by a crown of flowers, evidently won the first prize. The track of 88 spaces is decorated with scenes of various incidents on the journey to the parade. The enthusiasm for cycling as a means of transport in Holland is very apparent in this game – but it does not always go well. At space 9, you must stop one turn to repair your bike. At space 23 you can take a rest, with a drink and a pipe of tobacco, but must wait until another player arrives to take your place. Nor is traveling in a wagon free from mishap: at space 49, your waggon has knocked down a pedestrian and you must go back four spaces, also missing a turn for driving recklessly. In contrast, at space 25, you have won the second-prize for your float and may have your points again. Unusually, if a throw brings you right behind another player, you may jump over that player, who has to start the game afresh.

Carousel Game.
Amsterdam: Jos. Vas Dias
1889

As well as being a charming scene of children enjoying a fairground ride, the *Carousel* game is highly innovative. One unusual feature is that the game starts by players bidding to become the *pachter*, the man who rents the carousel. He is the figure standing on the right, with his purse, where he collects one counter from any player who lands on any of the red numbers. The counters accumulated there go to the player who made the highest bid at the start. The counters from that bid go to start the winner's pot, on the central seven. That pot is increased as each player must pay one counter to it on every turn. A second innovation is that two dice are used but their points are multiplied to determine the move, instead of being added as usual. Overthrows of the winning space, number 37, are therefore highly likely. The excess points are carried back to the start, unlike the reverse overthrows of the Goose game, so that the player really does go round and round, like the carousel. Also, if a player's token is hit by another, that player must start again. This game obviously taught children some useful arithmetic. It also taught them to judge their bets well, against expectations of the length of the game, a long game being much to the advantage of the *pachter*. Whether this was a good preparation for life depends on one's point of view.

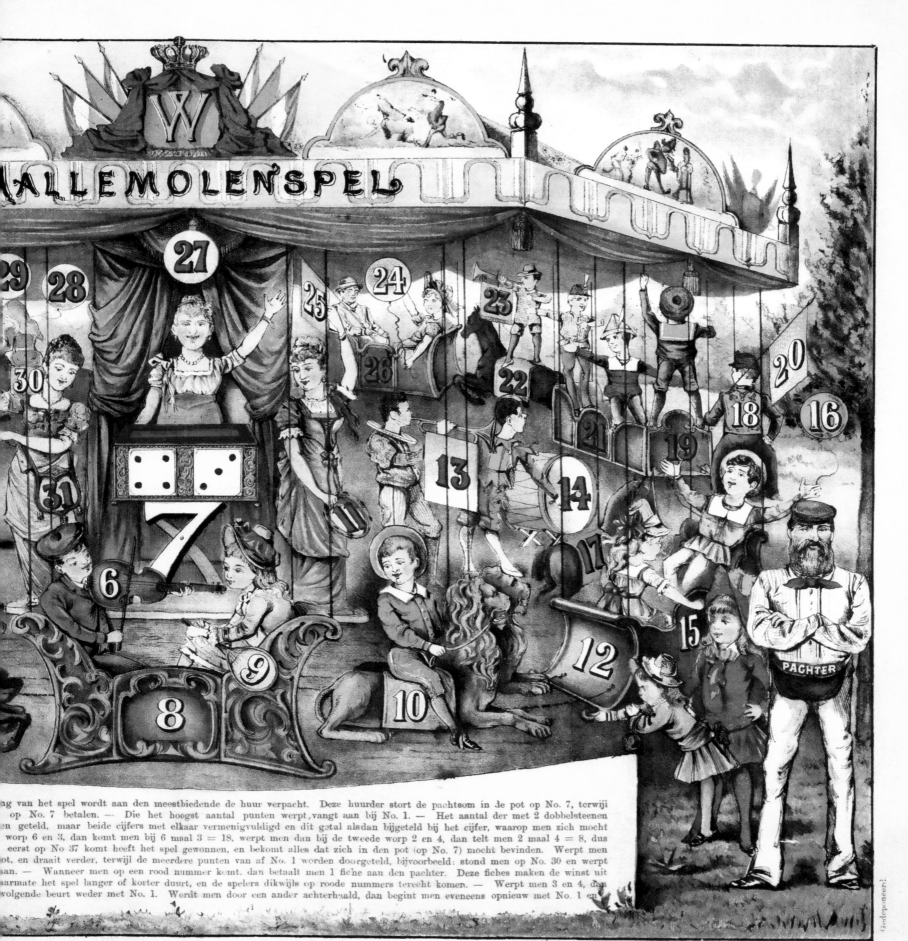

MALLEMOLENSPEL

...ng van het spel wordt aan den meestbiedende de huur verpacht. Deze huurder stort de pachtsom in de pot op No. 7, terwijl
... op No. 7 betalen. — Die het hoogst aantal punten werpt, vangt aan bij No. 1. — Het aantal der met 2 dobbelsteenen
... geteld, maar beide cijfers met elkaar vermenigvuldigd en dit getal alsdan bijgeteld bij het cijfer, waarop men zich mocht
... worp 6 en 3, dan komt men bij 6 maal 3 = 18, werpt men dan bij de tweede worp 2 en 4, dan telt men 2 maal 4 = 8, dus
... eerst op No 37 komt heeft het spel gewonnen, en bekomt alles dat zich in den pot (op No. 7) mocht bevinden. Werpt men
... ot, en draait verder, terwijl de meerdere punten van af No. 1 worden doorgeteld, bijvoorbeeld: stond men op No. 30 en werpt
... aan. — Wanneer men op een rood nummer komt, dan betaalt men 1 fiche aan den pachter. Deze fiches maken de winst uit
... aarmate het spel langer of korter duurt, en de spelers dikwijls op roode nummers terecht komen. — Werpt men 3 en 4, dan
... volgende beurt weder met No. 1. Wordt men door een ander achterhaald, dan begint men eveneens opnieuw met No. 1 en

Nieuw Vermakelijk Mallemolenspel."

Lith. Jos. Vas Dias & Co. Amsterdam.

Game of the Giant Wheel of Paris. Paris: Fabrique S. C. 1900

The Giant Wheel was erected in 1899 for the *Exposition Universelle*, a world's fair held in Paris from 14 April to 12 November 1900 to celebrate the achievements of the past century and to look forward into the next. At 106 meters (348 ft) high, it was the tallest panoramic wheel built to that date, much taller than the original Chicago Ferris Wheel, built for the 1883 World's Columbian Exhibition. It had 40 carriages, each carrying 40 passengers. Using a picture of the wheel as the basis for a board game meant that the 63 spaces of the Goose game were too many. The designer compromised by having 40 spaces on the wheel but made the start at the lower left before moving onto the wheel, then added three spaces on flags in the center, and made a winning space at the lower right. The traditional hazards are all present but the *prison* has been moved to space 22 and *death* to space 38. Given these concessions to the Goose-game model, it seems odd that no points-doubling spaces are provided. Perhaps the splendid graphics of the game were considered to be all the excitement necessary. Certainly, the decorations in the spaces of the track are lively, some showing important buildings in Paris, including the newly-constructed Eiffel Tower, both in real form and – at space 3 – being built with some considerable optimism as a sandcastle.

141

Cycle Sport Game. Amsterdam: Vlieger

1891

The illustrations in the Cycle Sport Game offer snapshots of cycling development in 1891. Here we have not only racing 'penny-farthing' machines, with their attendant dangers, but also more sedate three-wheelers of several different geometries. Here, too, are all kinds of headgear, from jockeys' caps to a fine top-hat – and the sport is clearly enjoyed by both sexes and by cyclists of a wide range of ages. The game is a re-interpretation of the Goose game, using two opposing tracks to be negotiated by opposing teams, red and blue. The initial throw of nine means that you are either Champion of the Netherlands, or Champion of the World, and may advance correspondingly to space 21 or 42 on your assigned track. The favorable spaces, doubling your points, are denoted by images of single cycles. A collision means that you start again, whereas a broken or faulty machine loses a turn. The ladies' cycle, post cycle and water cycle require you to wait until another joins you. Of these, the water cycle looks entirely fanciful but is in fact very like the Pinkert Navigating Tricycle, invented in 1891, on which the inventor managed to get half-way across the English Channel before needing to be rescued by a passing ship.

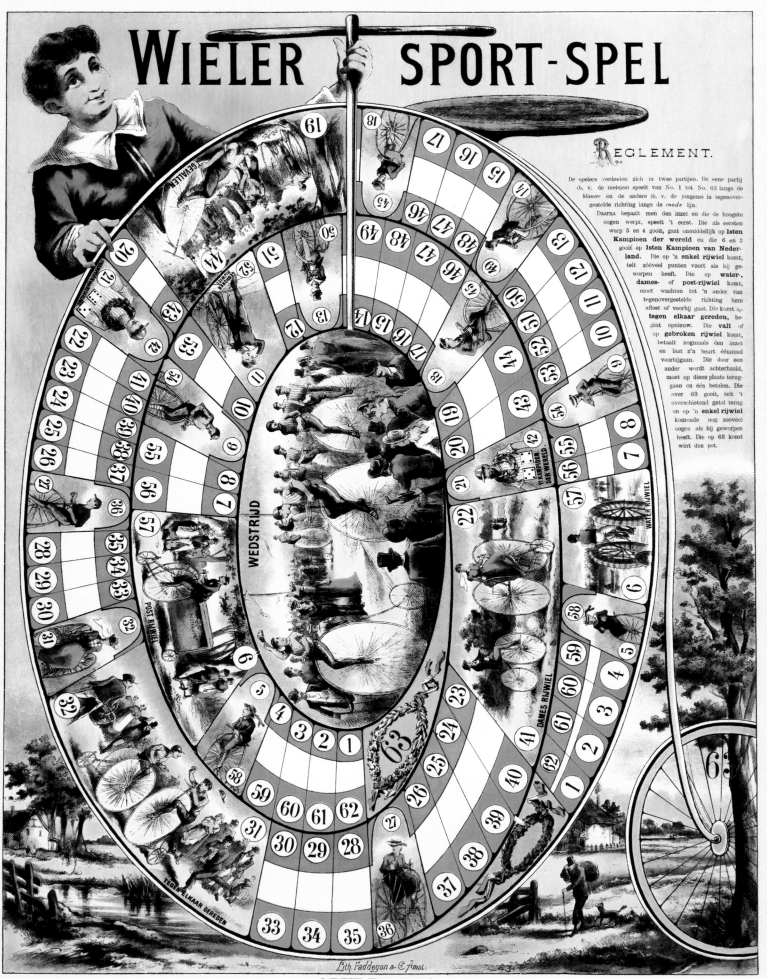

WIELER SPORT-SPEL

Lith. Faddegon & C? Amst.

J. VLIEGER, Uitgever, Amsterdam.

143

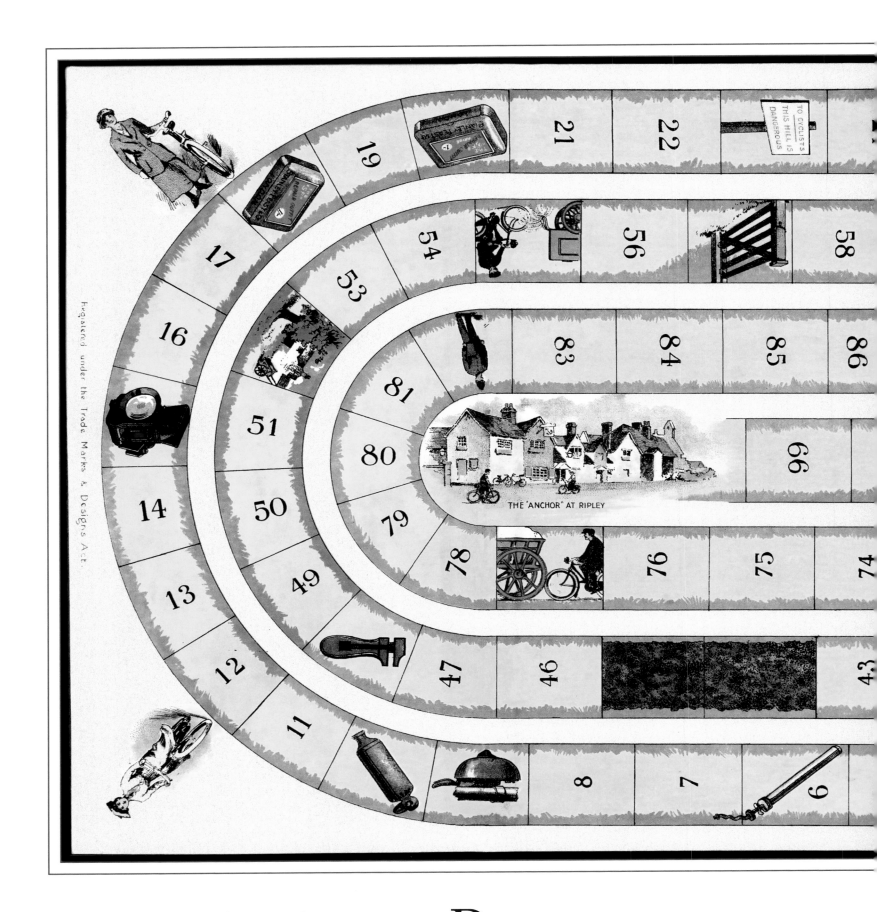

Wheeling. London: Jaques

1900

By the turn of the century, cycling technology was well advanced, with the introduction of the 'safety bicycle', and cycling had become a weekend diversion for the masses. A favorite destination for cyclists from London was The Anchor, which was (and still is) a public house at Ripley, a village in Surrey on the road to Portsmouth, 22 miles southwest of London. The game of *Wheeling* makes this convenient and

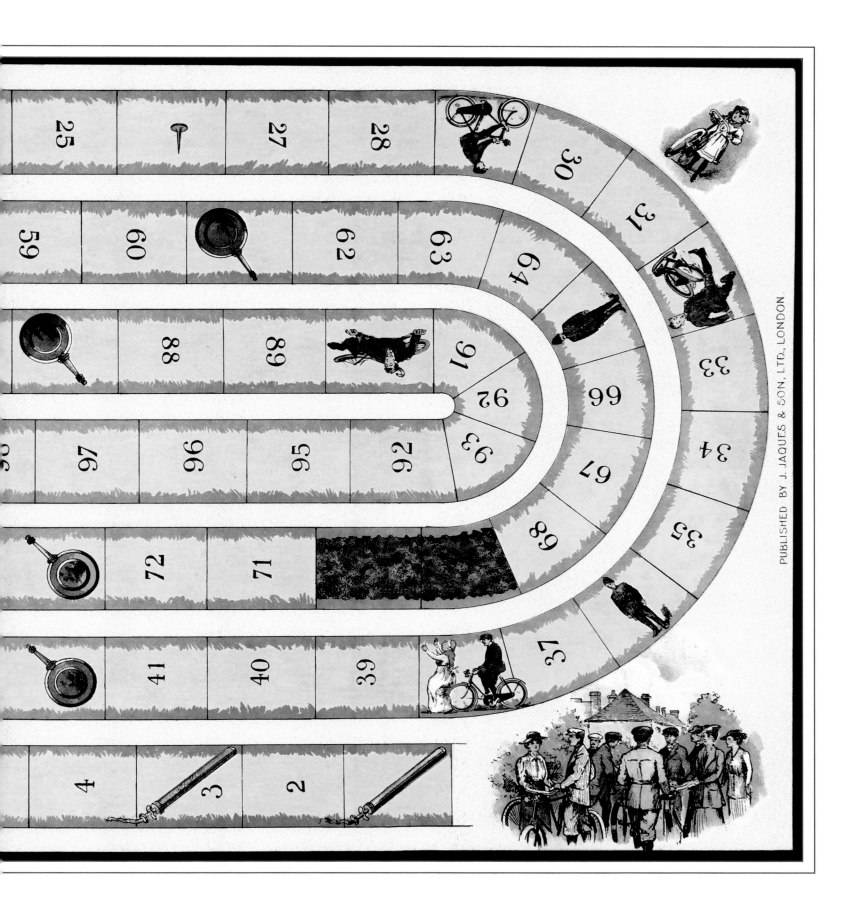

PUBLISHED BY J. JAQUES & SON. LTD. LONDON.

scenic ride its theme, depicting The Anchor at its winning space. The player has to throw 1, 3 or 6 with one die in order to start and 'pump up his tyres'; thereafter, two dice are used. The game, though not obviously derived from the Game of the Goose, is like it in having a regular sequence of favorable spaces, e.g., at each oil-can, a player can move on five more spaces. On the early part of the track are spaces that entitle the player to receive a 'ticket' (one of a set of printed cards supplied with the game) for a bell or whistle, for a pneumatic outfit, or for a lamp. These tickets enable the player to avoid being penalized at later hazards, such as at space 26 (a sharp tack), where unless provided with a pneumatic outfit the player must go back to space 10 and get one. But one hazard is final: space 90, where the player smashes his machine and has to retire from the game.

On the Ice. Paris: Saussine

about 1900

Like the previous game, *Sur la Glace* [On the Ice] is an elegant chromolithograph produced by the firm of Saussine, one of the major French manufacturers of games between its founding in 1860 and closure in the 1960s. Their games were often original (the founder, Léon Saussine, held several patents) and were always attractive. As well as catering for the French market, they aimed at an international clientele, frequently printing their rule sheets in both French and English, while avoiding text on the game board itself. Here, though, a rule sheet is hardly necessary, for the game is simplicity itself. The parallel tracks of the toboggans serve instead of ladders, up or down according to the direction indicated so graphically by the figures of the children enjoying their sport. There is, though, the occasional snowball heading down towards a snowman, just for variety. Like the English *Snakes and Ladders* from which it derives, this game has 100 spaces arranged on a back-and-forth rectangular track. However, the ups and downs do not correspond to those of the parent game. In particular, there is no really long descent from any of the spaces near the end, something that would have given extra spice to the game, comparable to the *death* space in the Game of the Goose. Perhaps the designer felt that this would have spoiled the balance of the layout.

147

Satire and Polemic: Games with a Bite!

Thise games are not for children. The French were particularly fond of games based on political intrigues such as the Dreyfus case but other countries too enjoyed these witty adult pursuits.

Most of the games in this chapter are from France, where satirical and polemical games have a long tradition, dating back to the end of the seventeenth century, when a game satirizing the complexities and frustrations of the legal system appeared. That game had as its goal the workhouse, *to which the hapless litigant was reduced by the expenses and reversals of pleading a case at law. To make the point absolutely clear, unlike in the Game of the Goose, here there were no favorable spaces at all.*

This chapter begins with a game chronicling the French Revolution, making many satirical allusions to the Ancien Régime *which had been overthrown. But next there comes a game whose hidden aim is to cement the restoration of* the Bourbon monarchy. *In fact, all the stages of France's stormy history in the nineteenth century were marked by the appearance of board games with strong political content. For example, the transition to the Third Republic in 1870 after the collapse of Second Empire, gave rise to the elaborate* Parliamentary Game of the Goose, *a game of clear satirical intent, which was mocking parliamentary customs even before the new regime was properly established. The* Game of Laws, *which was published about the same time in the satirical magazine* Charivari, *was in a similar vein, though here the emphasis was in retrospective condemnation of the Second Empire under Napoleon III.*

Apart from the continuing turmoil in France, the nineteenth century saw much political change in the rest of Europe. The unification of Italy gave rise, in its early stages, to an insightful game, Italy in the nineteenth century. *It, too, was published in a satirical journal, but in this game the* feeling is of patriotism and hope for the new Italy, looking back with approval to the influential figures of the past who had helped the revolutionary cause. In France, the years at the turn of the nineteenth century were animated by intense political debate, triggered by the Dreyfus affair. In 1894, Captain Alfred Dreyfus, a young artillery officer of Jewish descent, had been convicted of treason for passing French military secrets to the German Embassy in Paris. Only after nearly five years of imprisonment on Devil's Island in French Guiana was he found to have been falsely accused. The scandal, which divided political opinion in France, gave rise in 1898 to the publication of a highly-charged game, The Dreyfus Affair and the Truth, where the injustice and hypocrisy of the authorities were put to scorn.

Another highly charged game brought to public attention the scandals of the 'Humbert affair': one of the greatest scams of all time. Thérèse Humbert, a peasant girl from the Languedoc, had a remarkable tale to tell. She claimed that in 1879 she had helped a wealthy American who had been taken ill on a train and that, as a reward, he had promised her a rich inheritance. On the strength of this, she borrowed large sums of money and lived a life of luxury in Paris for almost twenty years. The Game of the Rabbit of La Grande Therese not only chronicles her rise and fall but also ridicules the credulous persons whom she deceived so successfully, several of whom were in high official positions.

In England, there was also political turmoil at this time – but here it centered on the campaign to get women the vote. The game of Pank-a-Squith is a rare example of an English political board game of the race type. On a background of the adopted colors of the Suffragette movement, purple and green, the game chronicles the bitter struggle faced by the Suffragettes in their militant but unsuccessful campaign. Not until after the Great War did women get the vote in England.

Game of the French Revolution.
Paris: publisher unknown
1790

This game promotes the ideals and achievements of the French Revolution. Every space is illustrated, forming a history of the earliest months of the Revolution, beginning with the Storming of the Bastille (14 July 1789) and ending at winning space 63 with the National Assembly at the Palladium of Liberty. The favorable *Goose* spaces celebrate the abolition of the *Parlements*. These courts of law, set up in medieval times, had resisted reforms, such as changes that would have made the nobility pay more tax. As bastions of reaction and privilege, all of them were quickly abolished by the Revolution. They are marked in the game by satirical caricatures of geese dressed as lawyers, described in the rules as *oies bridées* [nincompoops]. The hazard spaces are also satirically transformed. For example, the *labyrinth* at space 42 shows the Châtelet of Paris, an important law court – implying that Justice is hard to find there. Space 58 shows the death of Delaunay, Foulon, Berthier etc. The Marquis de Launay was Governor of the Bastille and was lynched by the mob after it was stormed. Foulon was appointed Controller of Finances in 1789 and was much hated: he tried to escape from Paris but was captured and beheaded by the crowd, together with his son-in-law Berthier. His head was paraded on a pike, his mouth stuffed with hay, as illustrated in the game. He had unwisely said that the people should eat hay if they were hungry.

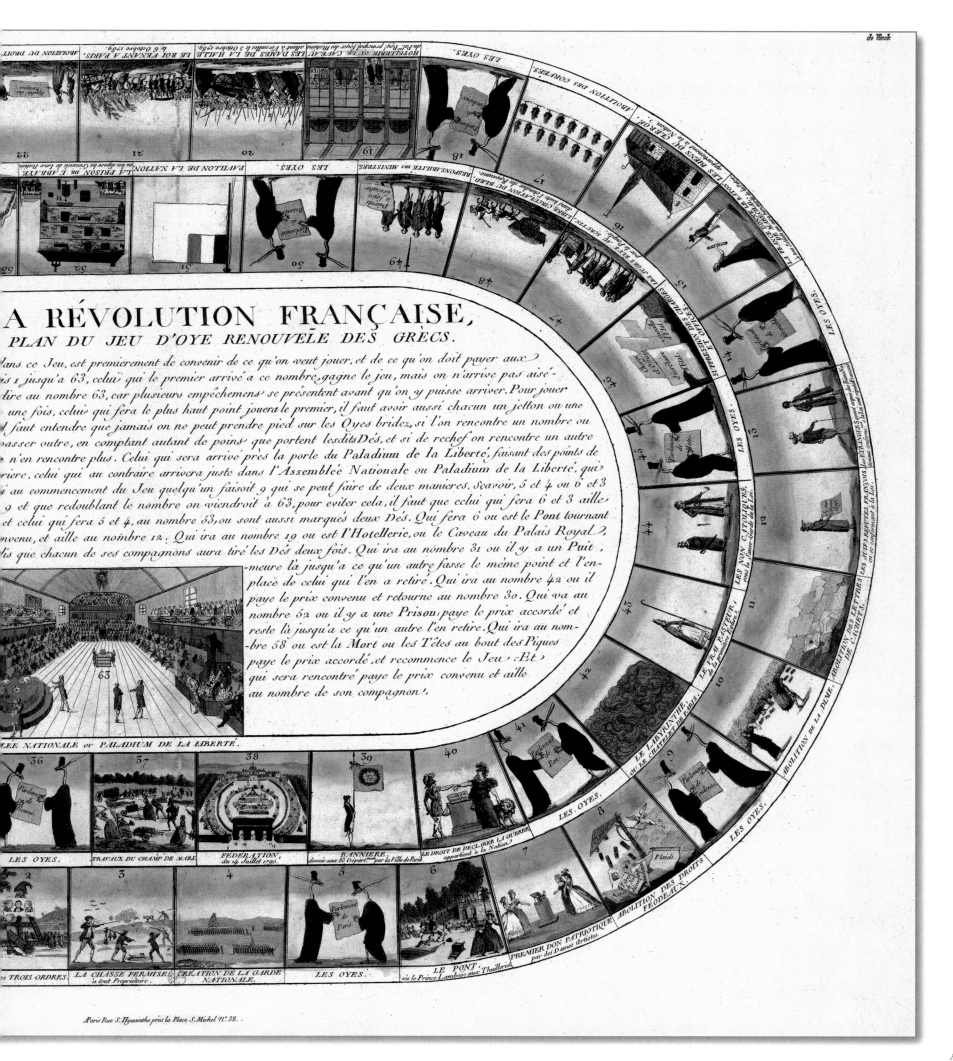

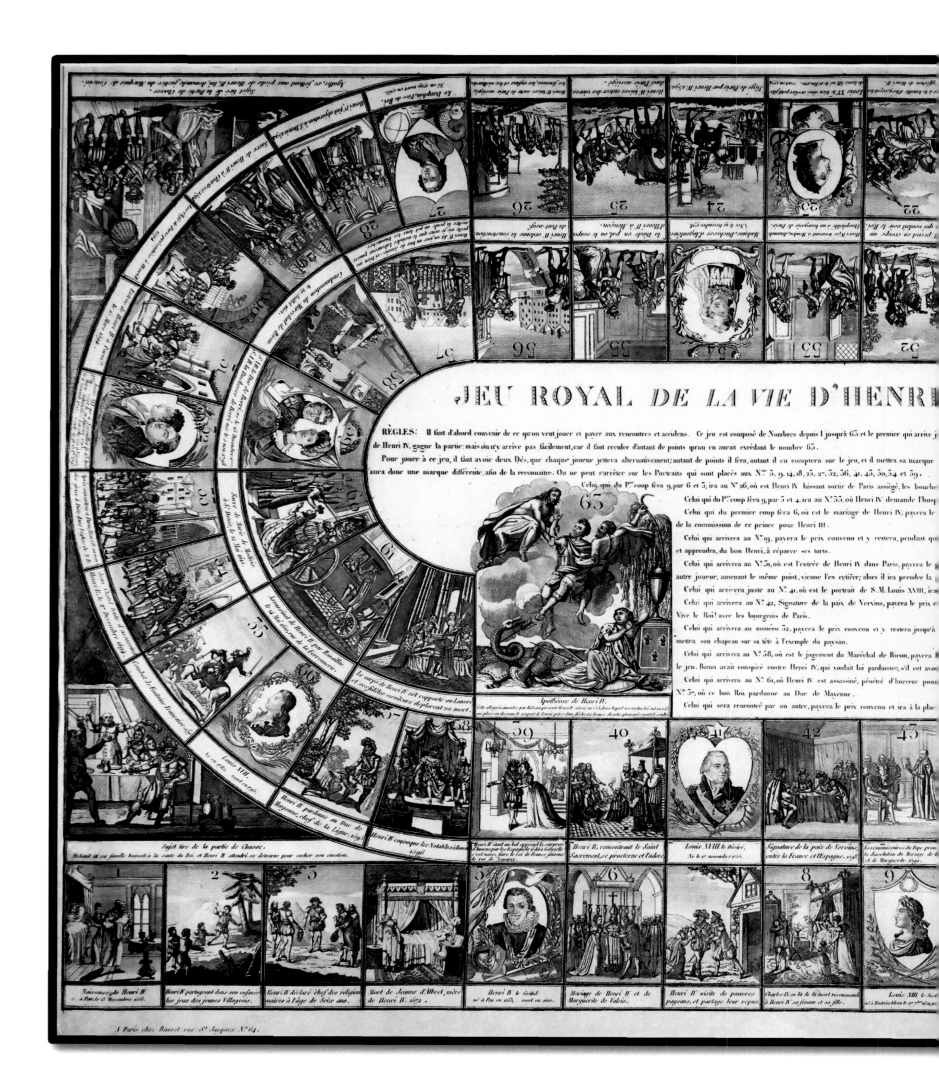

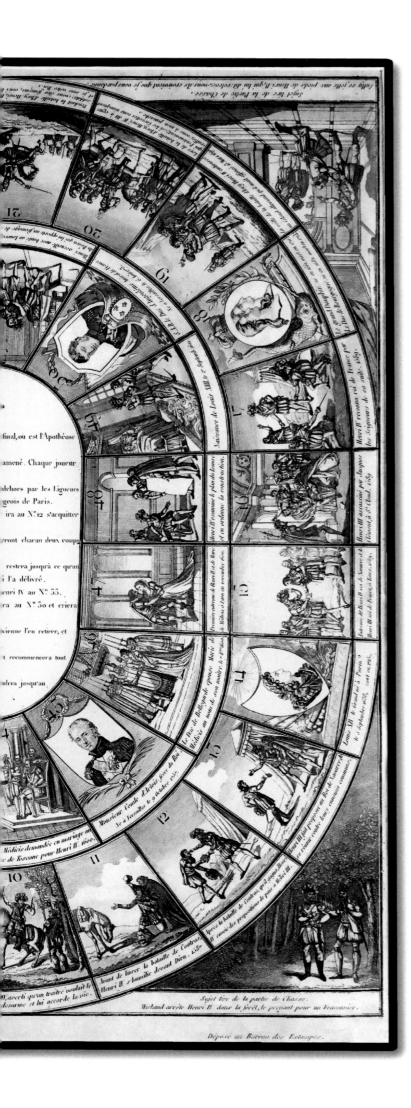

Royal Game of the Life of Henri IV.
Paris: Basset
1815

The *Royal Game of the Life of Henri IV* looks at first sight to be a straightforward historical game chronicling the life of this popular monarch, who is said to have promised every Frenchman 'a chicken in the pot'. The game shows scenes from Henri's life, beginning with his birth in 1553 and ending with his assassination at space 61. The winning space at 63 shows his ascent to heaven, as depicted by Rubens. In fact, though, this is a game with a subtle political message. It celebrates the Bourbon Restorations, which brought Louis XVIII to the throne of France following the fall of Napoleon. It is a largely classic Goose game, in which all the favorable spaces depict members of the new royal house. The propaganda message is that Henry's good name will in some way sanctify the Restoration. A special rule governs space 41, which portrays Louis XVIII himself: 'go to dine with Henri IV' at space 55, which shows Henri before a large fireplace in which a turkey is roasting for his supper. A good (if legendary) story relates that Henri, before the Battle of Ivry, arrived incognito at an officer's house in Alençon, where the wife did not recognize him. Lacking anything to give him for dinner, she acquired a turkey from a neighbor, who joined them for the meal. The neighbor was the local wit and so delighted Henri with his conversation that he ennobled him – issuing him with a coat of arms showing a turkey on a spit.

Parliamentary

Game of the Goose.

Paris: Vancortenberghen

1871

RÉGLE DU JEU DE LA DROITE.

BELLOGUET DEL. & LITH.

The large and imposing *Parliamentary Game of the Goose* provides portraits of the important French politicians of the day, accompanied by satirical vignettes. In this distinctive game, the 'left' is pitted against the 'right': each side plays upon its own game track of 50 spaces, the aim of the 'left' being to arrive at the final space, marked *changement du cabinet* [change of government] before the 'right' reach their final space, marked *Vote de confiance* [vote of confidence]. The game represents the French legislative assembly, taking the form of a semicircle divided into two parts, like the Chamber. At the center is placed the platform supporting the traditional glass of sugar-water for speakers and below the platform, the seat of the President, with his little bell for controlling the debates. The assembly seems to have been a rowdy affair, with murmuring, whistles, protests, noisy laughter and interruptions of many kinds. The rules, which are different for the two sides, are incomplete, or at least hard to interpret in playing terms, suggesting that this sheet was intended more for satirical amusement than to be played as a game.

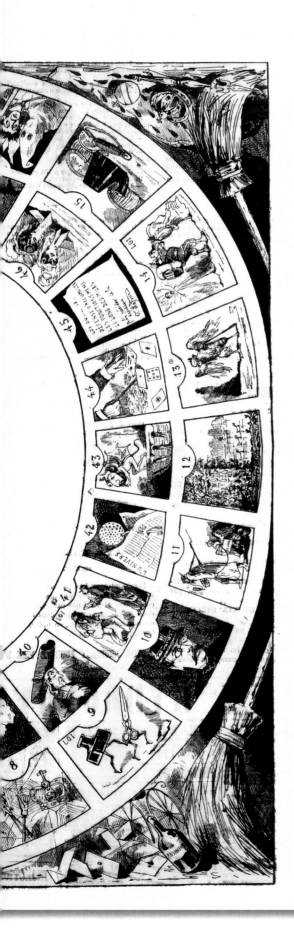

The *Game of Laws* is a satire against the Second Empire, which had ended in the fall of Napoleon III. The flavor is indicated in the upper left corner, which shows a choice of masks for politicians to hide their true nature, together with a phrase book of 'fine words for high officials', all being swept away by a large broom. Various laws to be passed by the new administration are advocated on the Goose spaces. Particular hatred is shown against Otto von Bismark, Chancellor of the German Empire from 1871, who was a key figure in bringing about the Franco-Prussian war in 1870, in which France suffered serious defeats. His reward is that he is featured on the *death* space. But former emperor Napoleon III fares little better – his image is on space 60, in a fine uniform. The game rule says that when you arrive there: 'you will recoil so quickly that you will not stop until you get to space number 1'. There is condemnation too, for the Commune, a radical left-wing government formed when Paris workers and the National Guard revolted in March 1871 – it is symbolized by a container full of petrol at space 62, in reference to petrol bombs at the barricades. Only the Republic is approved, as shown on the winning space.

Italy in the 19th Century.
Milan: La Cicala Politica
1861

An important phase of the unification of Italy was marked by the publication on 25 February 1861 of a patriotic version of a Game of the Goose on a sheet inserted in the satirical journal *La Cicala Politica*, Milan. *Italy in the 19th century, or the newest Game of the Goose*, to give it its full title, features figures thought to be instrumental in bringing about political change. These 'celebrated Italians' act as goose spaces, doubling the points thrown. Here are writers such as Giacomo Leopardi and Ugo Foscolo; generals Napoleon Bonaparte and Guglielmo Pepe; the Nationalist brothers Attilio and Emilio Bandiera, whose martyrdom in 1844 gave a moral lead to the uprisings that followed. Here, too, are the important figures of Vittorio Emmanuele II and Count Cavour, though Mazzini is nowhere to be seen. Spaces on the track are separated by significant images – for example, the Papal Slipper between spaces 52 and 53, lettered '*concordato*' [agreement]. The prison space is represented by the Castle of Spielberg, where many Carbonari (revolutionaries) were held prisoner by the Austro-Hungarian regime. The equivalent of the *death* space is Diplomacy, at number 46 - start again. At the winning space stand Garibaldi and Victor Emmanuel, saluting a flag with the slogan: 'Italy for the Italians'.

L'ITALIA DEL SECOLO DECIMONONO
OSSIA
IL NUOVISSIMO GIUOCO DELL'OCA
INVENTATO DA PUFF E DISEGNATO DA DON CICCIO.

NOTE DELL'AUTORE.

Questo giuoco è composto di 61 numeri, ed a giuocare si fa in questo modo:

Si pigliano due dadi numerati dall'uno al sei cadauno, indi si fa chi debba tirare pel primo, e si mette la moneta convenuta.

Chi va al 6, dove sonvi i Franco-Muratori, salta al 19, dove trovansi i Carbonari, ma paga la posta.

Chi capita al 15, ossia alla Santa Alleanza, torna da capo il giuoco pagando la posta.

Chi arriva al 21 casca nello Spielbergo, paga e vi sta rinchiuso senza più tirare finchè un altro porero disgraziato, arrivando allo stesso numero, lo cavi e vi resti in suo luogo pagando il convenuto. Il primo ch'era nello Spielbergo andrà al posto dov'era il secondo.

Chi fa di primo giuoco 6 e 3, o 5 e 4 salta addirittura ai così detti numeri d'onore, che sono il 31 pel 6 e 3, ed il 48 pel 5 e 4.

Chi capita al 36 e s'incontra nel Cholera, paga la posta e scappa subito indietro a' posto di prima.

Chi casca nel 49, ossia nella Diplomazia, bisogna che torni irremissibilmente da capo il giuoco pagando la posta.

Chi va nel 56 in Crimea paga la posta, è vero, ma ha il vantaggio di tirare una seconda volta.

Capitando nel 59 a Villafranca, non si paga la posta, ma si sta tre giri senza giuocare per riaversi dallo stupore.

Il primo che arriva al 61 porta via tutto, ma chi lo oltrepassa torna indietro.

Imbattendosi nei celebri italiani (numeri 5, 9, 14, 18, 23, 27, 32, 41, 45, 50, 54) si va sempre avanti come nel giuoco dell'oca.

PROPRIETA' DEL GIORNALE LA CICALA POLITICA.

159

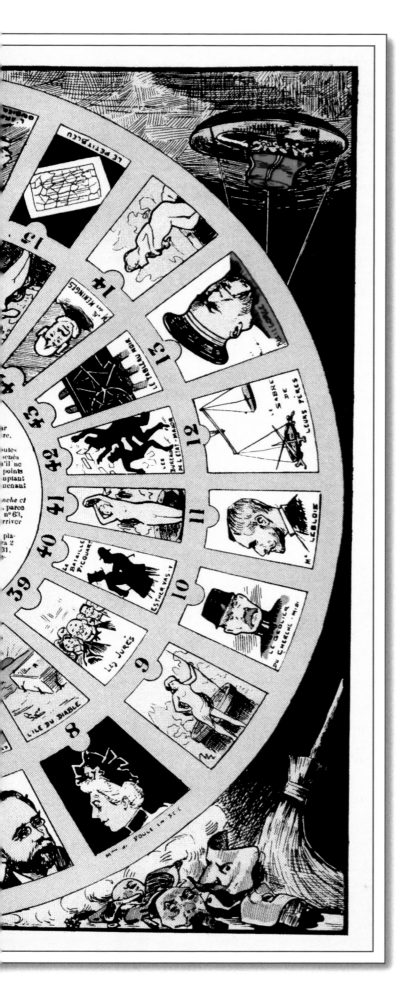

*T*he *Dreyfus Affair and the Truth* was a game published in 1898 by the French journal *L'Aurore*, highlighting the injustices of the Dreyfus Affair. The game is a variant of the classic Game of the Goose, with the figure of 'Truth' replacing the geese. The object is to arrive at space 63, showing 'the naked truth'. Spaces 24 and 21 are caricatures of the President of the Court that had tried Dreyfus, and of the Procurator General. Space 52 shows the military prison of Cherche-Midi in Paris, where Dreyfus was confined in 1894. Space 31 shows the prison of Mont Valérien, where Hubert-Joseph Henry, a Lieutenant-Colonel in army intelligence, was confined in 1898, having been arrested for forging evidence against Dreyfus. He cut his throat with a razor, taking to the grave his secret. The real traitor was eventually shown to be a certain Major Ferdinand Esterhazy. He had falsely claimed that a mysterious 'veiled lady' had given him a photograph of a document 'proving' Dreyfus's guilt. The death space, number 58, shows the 'death' of the veiled lady, a personage entirely invented by Esterhazy. The cartoon style of the drawing greatly enriches the satire – for example, space 42, the offices of the Military General Staff, shows two officers arguing fiercely, with papers flying in all directions.

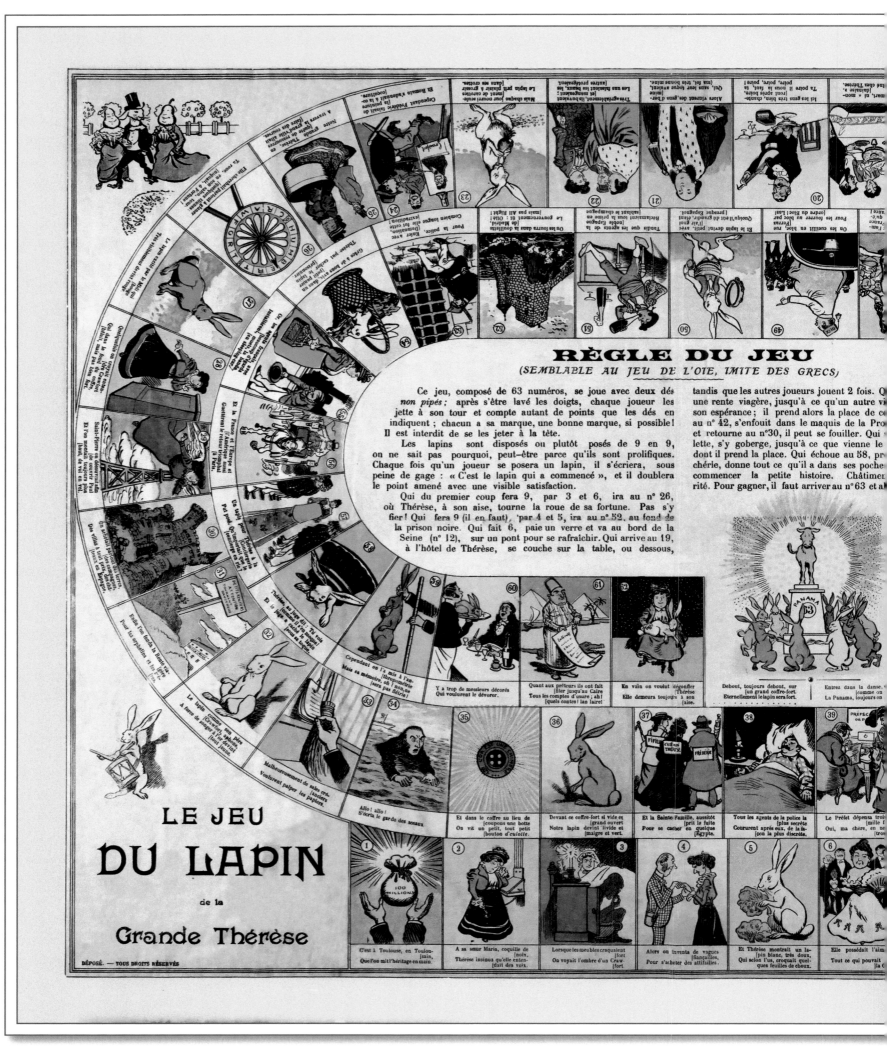

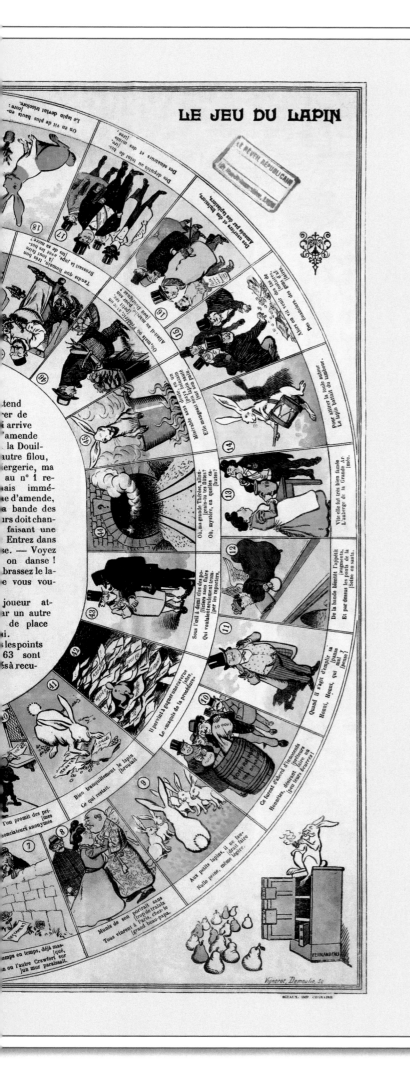

Game of the Rabbit of La Grande Thérèse. Sceaux: Charaire

1901

The *Game of the Rabbit of La Grande Thérèse* also benefits from the cartoon style. Here the artist is Fernand Fau, a widely published French illustrator, whose cartoons unfold the story of Thérèse Humbert and her great deception. The instructions begin satirically by saying that the game is to be played with two dice, *without pips*. The rabbits, which appear on every ninth space, act as Goose spaces: they are not explained on the sheet but, in French slang of the period, when a person got the worst of a bargain he was said 'to have bought the rabbit,' a phrase derived from an old story about a man selling a cat to a foreigner for a rabbit. Here, though, the rabbit changes color alarmingly: at space 32 it has turned yellow, through dreaming of gold, and it multiplies prolifically. The death space at 58 shows the rabbit caught under a judge's *toque*, in reference to Thérèse's eventual conviction by the court, when she was sentenced to five years in prison with hard labor. The final space, at 63, shows variously-colored rabbits dancing round a statue of the Golden Calf, labeled 'Panama' in reference to an earlier corruption scandal, when in 1892 members of the French Government took bribes to hide the financial problems of the Panama Canal Company. The game satirizes the gullibility and greed of those who lost money in the scam.

Pank-a-Squith.

Manchester: Women's Social

and Political Union

about 1909

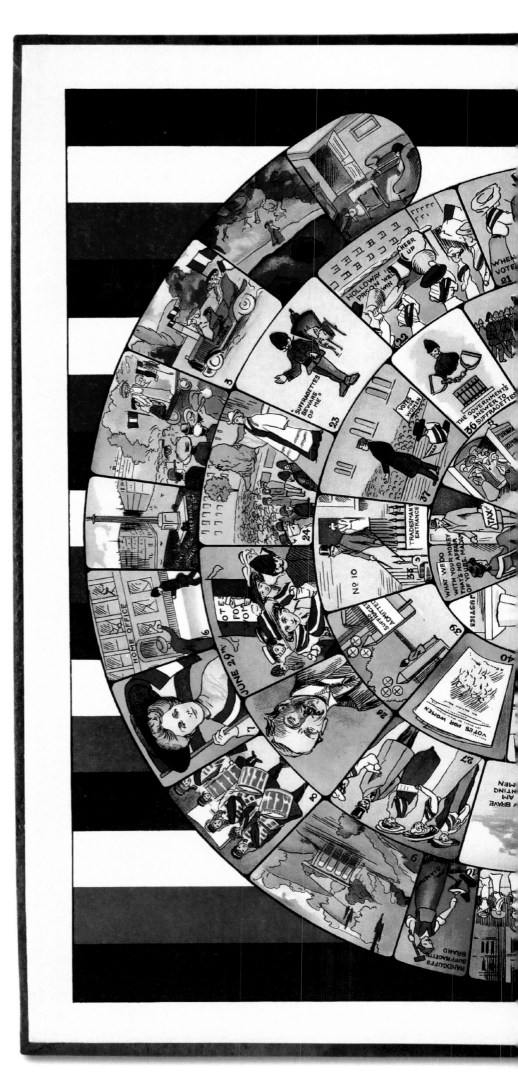

PANK-a-SQUITH

Within the board illustration:

DOWING ST

GREAT VOTES FOR WOMEN DEMONSTRATION

VOTES FOR WOMEN

PETITION OF RIGHTS WALL

FALLING GOVERNMENT

VOTES FOR WOMEN

HOLLOWAY

QUEENS HALL

CLEMENTS INN

VOTES FOR WOMEN

I WON'T EAT TILL I'M PLACED IN THE 1ER DIVISION

NOTICE :— Any player landing on this space must send a penny to the Suffragette Funds.

GREETING THE EX-PRISONER

INSPECTOR JARVIS

*P*ank-a-Squith derives its name from two of the chief political opponents of Edwardian England, the suffragette leader Emmeline Pankhurst (1858-1928) and Herbert Asquith, Prime Minister from 1908 to 1916. The spiral track illustrates the obstacles encountered by Mrs Pankhurst and her supporters in their militant campaign to establish the vote for women, the objective being space 50, the Houses of Parliament. The game can be dated to about 1909 by internal references. Thus, space 25 refers to the demonstration outside the Houses of Parliament on 29 June 1909 by members of the Women's Social and Political Union [WSPU], a women-only political movement campaigning for women's suffrage in the United Kingdom. Also, space 43 refers to forced feeding for hunger strikers, introduced in the same year. *Pank-a-Squith* was commissioned from an unknown German manufacturer to help raise funds for the WSPU. The designer was evidently not fully conversant with English usage - space 20 shows the Prime Minister's residence as 'Dowing Street' instead of 'Downing Street'. Perhaps because of the German connection, the game's detailed rules owe much to the Game of the Goose, though there is no regular sequence of favorable spaces. Space 32 (Holloway Prison, where many suffragettes were sent) acts as a *death* space (start again). Space 25 celebrates 'the brave deputation' of June 29th, when Mrs Pankhurst led a group of eight women to Parliament to present a petition to Mr Asquith. When he refused to receive them, Mrs. Pankhurst struck a police inspector. Outside Parliament, hundreds of suffragettes confronted police officers and began smashing windows. Afterwards, 107 women and eight men were arrested.

165

Advertising and Promotion: Games with a Message

Towards the end of the nineteenth century, color printing was cheap enough for giveaway advertising games to be economic. The Dutch were probably the first, advertising drinking chocolate, but the French soon followed.

Perhaps the earliest examples of promotional games were the 'flyers' produced by certain French newspapers and magazines at the time of the Paris Exposition Universelle of 1867, creating interest in this important world fair. Advertising games proper began to appear in the 1880s. Certainly among the earliest, and perhaps even the first, was a clever adaptation of a Game of the Tramway promoting the drinking chocolate of the Dutch firm, Van Houten. To turn this into a promotional game, all that was necessary was to add their slogan to an existing print, so that the expense of a new design was avoided. It must have been a success, because the firm almost immediately embarked on a full-scale advertising campaign using specially designed game sheets in full color, with versions both in Dutch and French, aiming for a wide European market.

By the time of the Paris Exposition Universelle of 1889, advertising using the Game of the Goose as a basis had reached a considerable level of sophistication. Thus, when the French firm of Jumeau chose this means to promote the sale of their up-market dolls, they took care to emphasize how much superior to cheap imported German dolls their products were. Their impressive game sheet, featuring the newly-constructed Eiffel Tower, was given away free, 'to be put on cardboard and kept as a souvenir of the exhibition'.

A different form of promotion occurred in the same year when the Paris newspaper Le Figaro issued a splendid four-page political supplement in the run-up to the French general election. All of the parties contesting the election were represented: Republicans, Monarchists, Bonapartists and (on the page displayed in this chapter) the Boulangists, who supported 'Le Général', Georges Ernest Jean-Marie Boulanger (1837–1891). A French general and politician with a strong military record, his popularity among the working classes reached a high point in January 1889, when it seemed that he might even lead a coup d'état.

But Boulanger procrastinated and his powerful enemies took advantage of the delay. His political activities came under investigation and the French government issued a warrant for his arrest. Before it could be executed, Boulanger fled, first to Brussels, then to London. After Boulanger's flight, support fell away, his party lost the elections and in 1891 he shot himself on the grave of his beloved mistress, in a Brussels cemetery.

As advertising using games became more widespread, designers began to increase the amount of information about the product that was included. A particularly successful example was the Game of La Couronne Gas Mantles, *advertising what is now an all-but forgotten technology but one which at the end of the nineteenth century was important in improving both domestic and street lighting.*

Other designers worked the product amusingly into the rules, as in the Ferro-China *game, where various throws recommend that the player should be fortified by a drink of this once-popular Italian medicinal tonic* digestif, *an alcoholic mixture made with iron compounds and extracts of the bark of plants of the cinchona genus ('china' in Italian), yielding quinine and other medicinal alkaloids.*

In a different vein, pure fantasy inspired the game issued by the Paris department store, Galeries Lafayette, *in 1906. The store built on the general enthusiasm for the new phenomenon of aviation by providing a game where an aeroplane took off from the roof of the store and flew over the monuments of Paris before undertaking a world tour. The plane then sped away from Earth towards the outer planets and the Sun, before returning to land safely on the same rooftop.*

In the Carillon de Flandres *game, advertising chicory as a coffee substitute, the main appeal is to children, made by decorating the track with pictures of animals, birds and amusing figures from the* commedia dell'arte. *But a much more direct appeal to children is made by the final example in this chapter, the* Game of Nutrix Dwarves, *where biscuits are the key to a story of fairy adventure. This takes us well into the twentieth century, showing how games can contribute to sophisticated marketing techniques.*

Game of the

Paris Exhibition.

Paris: La Vie Parisienne

1867

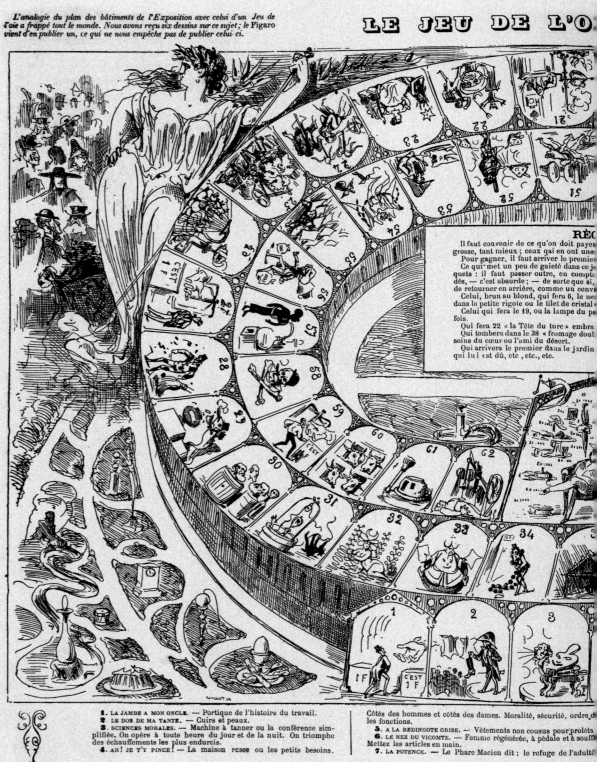

The *Exposition universelle d'art et d'industrie* [Universal Exhibition of Art and Industry] was staged in Paris in 1867, on the orders of Napoleon III. The intention was to out-do London's International Exhibition of 1862, which had not achieved the success of the Great Exhibition of 1851. The site chosen was the Champ de Mars, France's great military parade ground, and on this was erected the principal building, in the form of a rectangle with rounded-off ends, nearly 500 meters (1640 ft) in length. The outer ring of buildings enclosed several concentric smaller rings of the same shape. It was speedily recognized that this was uncannily like the shape of a Game of the Goose of the traditional French pattern. It was therefore not surprising that several Paris publications featured a Goose game as a representation of the exhibition itself. The version illustrated here, from the magazine *La Vie Parisienne*, was accompanied by articles about the exhibition, not entirely complimentary. One complaint was the charge for admission and this is reflected in the game, where the first rule says satirically that the initial stake is one franc: if you can pay more, so much the better; if you have less – too bad! The first space of the game shows a large money-grabbing hand extracting this charge from a visitor.

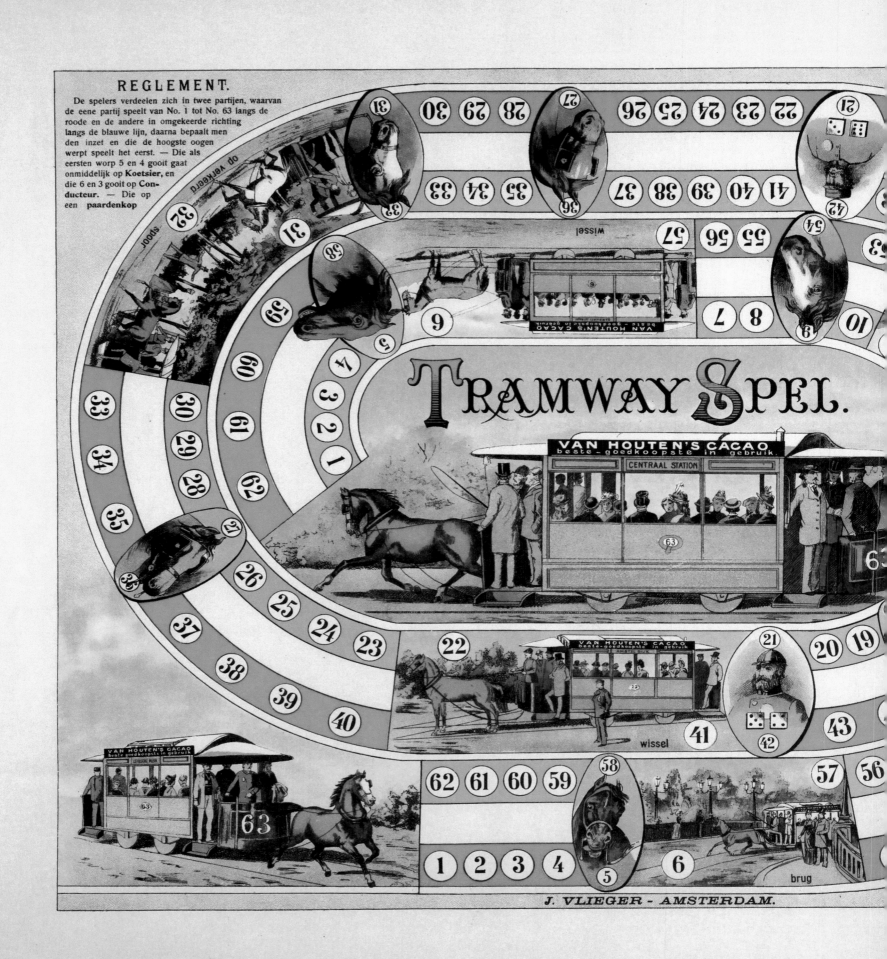

REGLEMENT.

De spelers verdeelen zich in twee partijen, waarvan de eene partij speelt van No. 1 tot No. 63 langs de roode en de andere in omgekeerde richting langs de blauwe lijn, daarna bepaalt men den inzet en die de hoogste oogen werpt speelt het eerst. — Die als eersten worp 5 en 4 gooit gaat onmiddelijk op **Koetsier**, en die 6 en 3 gooit op **Conducteur.** — Die op een **paardenkop**

TRAMWAY SPEL.

J. VLIEGER - AMSTERDAM.

komt telt zooveel punten voort als hij geworpen heeft. Die op de **brug** of **wissels** komt, moet wachten tot een ander van tegenovergestelde richting hem aflost of voorbijgaat. — Die op **verkeerd spoor** komt, begint opnieuw. — Die **derailleert** of op „**versche paarden**" komt betaalt nogmaals den inzet en laat zijn beurt éénmaal voorbijgaan. — Die door een ander wordt achterhaald moet op diens plaats teruggaan en één betalen. Die over **63** gooit telt het overschietende getal terug en op een **paarden-kop** komende nog zooveel oogen als hij geworpen heeft. Die op **63** komt wint den pot.

Game of the Tramway.

Amsterdam: Vlieger

about 1885

The *Tramway* game first appeared in about 1855, in France, and was highly popular, appearing in many editions in various countries. What makes this Dutch edition different and groundbreaking is the signboard on the tram: *Van Houten's Cacao*, with the advertising slogan 'best and cheapest in use', replacing the destination board in earlier editions. It is a two-track variant of the Game of Goose, played by two opposing teams of players. Here, one track is followed by the 'red' team while the 'blues' follow the other. The favorable goose-type spaces are indicated by horses' heads. The classic hazards are re-interpreted as problems that occur on the tramway. The *death* space becomes the 'wrong track' at 32 red /31 blue, where two trams meet head on. The *prison* and *well* hazards are here too, in the 'bridge' at 6/57 and 'crossing' at 41/22, where the player must wait until released by another from the opposing team. Waiting at a single-track bridge or a crossing point must have been all too familiar in real life. The delays of the *inn* and *labyrinth* spaces also have their counterparts: the tram is 'derailed' at 19/44 and 'fresh horses' are needed at 52/11. These ingenious changes made for a good, realistic game. The Tramway game remained popular over the years, being brought up to date with electrification.

Van Houten's Drinking Chocolate Game.

Weesp: Van Houten

1889

Like the *Game of the Tramway*, the *Drinking Chocolate Game* also advertised Van Houten's product and was likewise based on the traditional Game of Goose. The favorable spaces denoted by a goose in the original game were instead denoted by characteristic images of the Van Houten Cacao tin. As a further promotional device, the spaces without special playing significance spelled out the same advertising slogan as in the *Tramway* game. The promotional message was also reinforced by customizing the traditional hazard spaces: the *bridge* at space 6 was that of Weesp, a city in North Holland, the site of the Van Houten factory to the present day. Views of the city 'before' and 'because of' Van Houten were shown in the lower corners of the sheet. The *inn* at 19 became a cafe, while the *well* at 31 became one of van Houten's advertising trams. The *prison* at 52 was 'for counterfeiters' of the product, while the *death* space at 58 showed a coffee pot, where you must begin the game again 'for your recklessness' in choosing this unhealthy beverage.

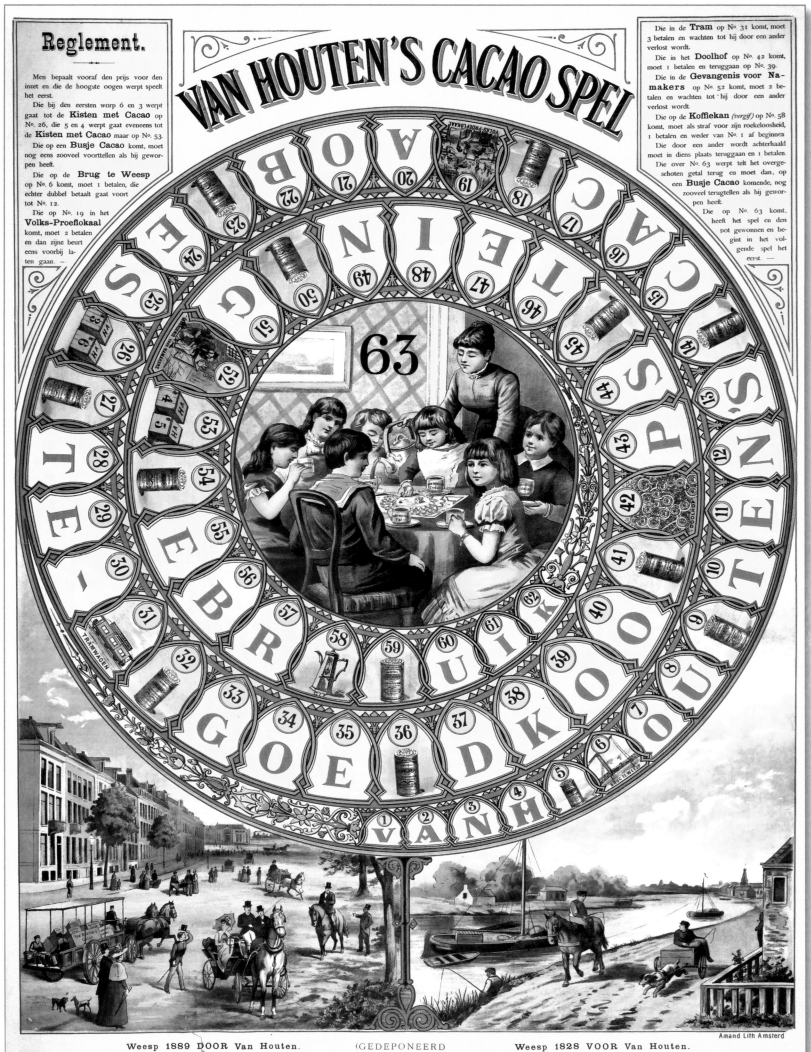

VAN HOUTEN'S CACAO SPEL

Reglement.

Men bepaalt vooraf den prijs voor den inzet en die de hoogste oogen werpt speelt het eerst.

Die bij den eersten worp 6 en 3 werpt gaat tot de **Kisten met Cacao** op No. 26, die 5 en 4 werpt gaat eveneens tot de **Kisten met Cacao** maar op No. 53.

Die op een **Busje Cacao** komt, moet nog eens zooveel voorttellen als hij geworpen heeft.

Die op de **Brug te Weesp** op No. 6 komt, moet 1 betalen, die echter dubbel betaalt gaat voort tot No. 12.

Die op No. 19 in het **Volks-Proeflokaal** komt, moet 2 betalen en dan zijne beurt eens voorbij laten gaan. —

Die in de **Tram** op No. 31 komt, moet 3 betalen en wachten tot hij door een ander verlost wordt.

Die in het **Doolhof** op No. 42 komt, moet 1 betalen en teruggaan op No. 39.

Die in de **Gevangenis voor Na-makers** op No. 52 komt, moet 2 betalen en wachten tot hij door een ander verlost wordt.

Die op de **Koffiekan** (vergif) op No. 58 komt, moet als straf voor zijn roekeloosheid, 1 betalen en weder van No. 1 af beginnen.

Die door een ander wordt achterhaald moet in diens plaats teruggaan en 1 betalen.

Die over No. 63 werpt telt het overge-schoten getal terug en moet dan, op een **Busje Cacao** komende, nog zooveel terugtellen als hij geworpen heeft.

Die op No. 63 komt, heeft het spel en den pot gewonnen en be-gint in het vol-gende spel het eerst. —

Weesp 1889 DOOR Van Houten. (GEDEPONEERD Weesp 1828 VOOR Van Houten.

Amand Lith Amsterd

173

Game of the Baby Jumeau Dolls. Paris: Jumeau 1889

The track of the *Game of the Baby Jumeau Dolls* is set out on a large image of the Eiffel tower, finishing at the top. The exhibition which the game records took place at a time of strong pro-American feeling in Paris, as indicated by the two flags at the top of the sheet and by New York's Statue of Liberty in the distant background. The game sheet also gives details of the firm of Jumeau: 'The large and beautiful factory at Montreuil, where the Jumeau Dolls come from, now covers 6000 sq m (65,000 sq ft) and employs 1000 staff...' Their dolls were made of bisque and wonderfully dressed in the elaborate fashions of the period, but were very expensive and suffered from competition against cheap imported German dolls. This struggle is reflected quite unashamedly in the game. The favorable spaces, on the traditional Goose numbers, show images of the Jumeau dolls. The unfavorable spaces are also themed. Most dramatic is the *death* space, on 58, where there is a broken German doll; the *prison* space, at 52, incarcerates another one, weeping piteously; and it is again a German doll who finds herself in the well, at 31, waiting for rescue. Though the firm is no more, the Jumeau dolls are much prized today by collectors and prices in five figures are realized for the rarest kinds.

Goose Game of General Boulanger. Paris: Figaro

1889

The illustration shows the first page of the full-color supplement executed for *Le Figaro* by the Imagerie Pellerin. The artist was Gaston Lucq (styling himself Glucq), a well-known Paris designer who, from the late 1880s, had been engaged by Charles Pellerin in a joint operation to produce modern advertising and political images. The *Goose Game of General Boulanger* appears below a spirited fan, showing the politicians of the General's party, dancing happily arm-in-arm. The game itself is of 63 spaces, with the goose spaces depicting the general himself, who is shown at the winning space wearing the imperial crown and dressed in robes of ermine. The hazards refer to incidents in his colorful career. For example, space 2 represents July 14 (Bastille Day) and celebrates his reintroducing the traditional military parades on that day, during his period of office as minister of war. Space 6, the lost 'portfolio', refers to his being sacked and sent to the provincial town of Clermont Ferrand by a government fearful of his rising popularity. His departure from the Gare de Lyon (space 12: go to space 44, Gare de Clermont) is duly noted. A mob of 10,000 of his supporters covered the train with posters that declared: 'He will return!' And indeed, space 44 itself has the instruction: 'Return to 12 (Gare de Lyon)'. The game would have raised a smile or two – perhaps the most effective form of political persuasion?

LE GÉNÉRAL   BOULANGER

REVUE DU 14 JUILLET 1886

Si je poussais à la guerre, je serais un fou ! Si je ne m'y préparais pas, je serais un misérable ! (Paroles du Général Boulanger.)

Commandant la division d'occupation de la Tunisie, il pacifie les tribus arabes. — Février 1884.

Éventail Boulangiste

RÈGLE DU JEU DE L'OIE DU GÉNÉRAL

Game of La Couronne Gas Mantles.
Paris: Robert and Co.
about 1900

This amusingly drawn game advertises the *La Couronne* brand of gas mantles, which were an important form of illumination before electric lighting became commonplace in the early twentieth century. The modern gas mantle was invented by Carl Auer von Welsbach, a German chemist who in 1891 perfected a mixture of rare-earth oxides that, when heated by burning gas, emitted a good white light from a relatively robust mantle. Every opportunity is taken in the game to emphasize the superiority of gas lighting over outdated forms of illumination - and indeed of the La Couronne mantles over their competitors. Space 7 shows *le bon achat*, a good buy, this being a pack of La Couronne mantles, so you double your throw. Space 31 is an accident due to using a bad mantle, showing the dramatic consequences and sending you back to buy a better product. Space 49 shows a terrified cat and its distressed owner following a similar mishap. Gas mantles were prone to sudden disintegration, with a loud bang, so the exaggeration is only slight. An engaging feature of the game is that the cone shape of the mantle is used to 'clothe' many of the human figures represented. The game is also of interest in showing the technology of production and use of gas mantles.

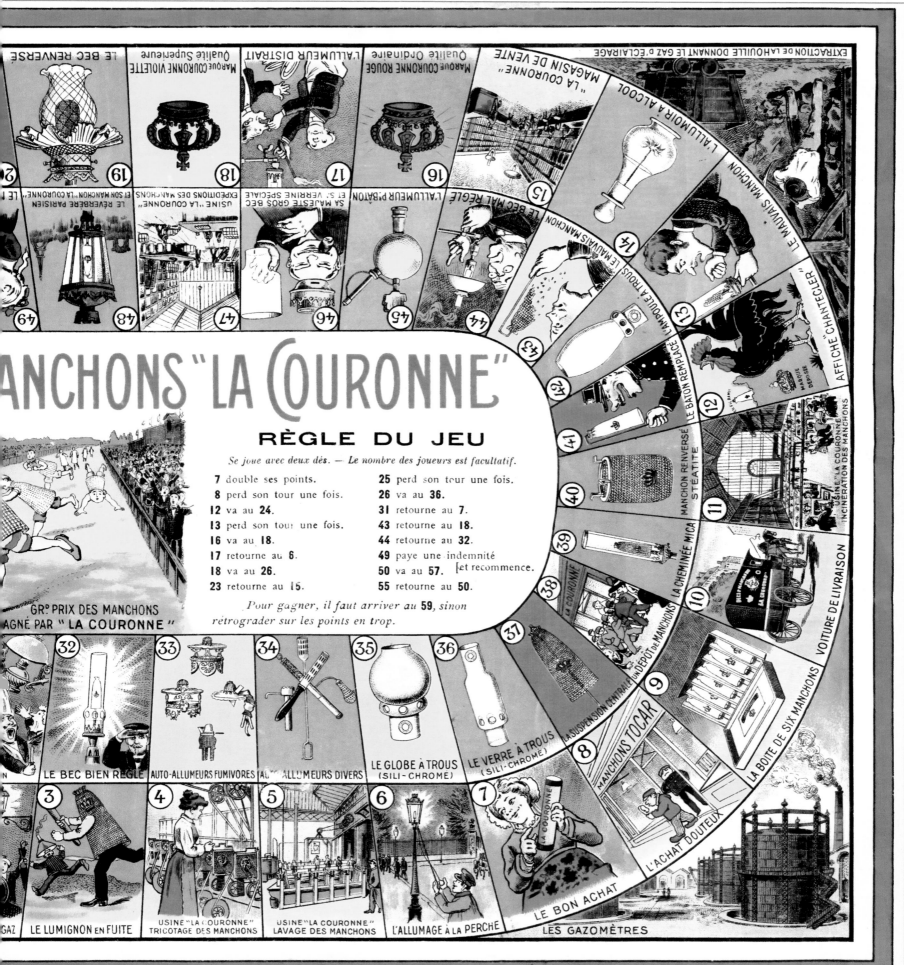

MANCHONS "LA COURONNE"

RÈGLE DU JEU

Se joue avec deux dés. — Le nombre des joueurs est facultatif.

7 double ses points.
8 perd son tour une fois.
12 va au **24**.
13 perd son tour une fois.
16 va au **18**.
17 retourne au **6**.
18 va au **26**.
23 retourne au **15**.

25 perd son tour une fois.
26 va au **36**.
31 retourne au **7**.
43 retourne au **18**.
44 retourne au **32**.
49 paye une indemnité et recommence.
50 va au **57**.
55 retourne au **50**.

*Pour gagner, il faut arriver au **59**, sinon rétrograder sur les points en trop.*

GR° PRIX DES MANCHONS GAGNÉ PAR "LA COURONNE"

LE BEC RENVERSÉ — MARQUE COURONNE VIOLETTE Qualité Supérieure — L'ALLUMEUR DISTRAIT — MARQUE COURONNE ROUGE Qualité Ordinaire — "LA COURONNE" MAGASIN DE VENTE — EXTRACTION DE LA HOUILLE DONNANT LE GAZ D'ÉCLAIRAGE

L'ALLUMOIR A ALCOOL — LE MAUVAIS MANCHON — AFFICHE "CHANTECLER"

LE RÉVERBÈRE PARISIEN ET SON MANCHON "LA COURONNE" — LE RÉVERBÈRE DES MANCHONS — USINE "LA COURONNE" EXPÉDITIONS DES MANCHONS — SA MAJESTÉ GROS BEC ET SA VERRINE SPÉCIALE — L'ALLUMEUR P'BATON — LE BEC MAL RÉGLÉ — LE MAUVAIS MANCHON — L'AMPOULE A TROUS — LE BATON REMPLACÉ — MANCHON RENVERSÉ STÉATITE — LA CHEMINÉE MICA — USINE "LA COURONNE" INCINÉRATION DES MANCHONS

LE BEC BIEN RÉGLÉ — AUTO-ALLUMEURS FUMIVORES — AUTO-ALLUMEURS DIVERS — LE GLOBE A TROUS (SILI-CHROME) — LE VERRE A TROUS (SILI-CHROME) — MANCHONS TOCAR — LA SUSPENSION CENTRALE D'UN DÉPÔT DE MANCHONS — VOITURE DE LIVRAISON — LA BOITE DE SIX MANCHONS

LE LUMIGNON EN FUITE — USINE "LA COURONNE" TRICOTAGE DES MANCHONS — USINE "LA COURONNE" LAVAGE DES MANCHONS — L'ALLUMAGE A LA PERCHE — LE BON ACHAT — L'ACHAT DOUTEUX — LES GAZOMÈTRES

Étab⁺⁵ ROBERT & C⁺⁵, 55 & 57, Rue Louis-Blanc, PARIS

Game of Bisleri Ferro-China tonic. Milan: Bisleri

about 1900

Bisleri's Ferro-China was created by Felice Bislieri, who in addition to making liqueurs was a pharmacist and a freedom fighter under Garibaldi. The game of the Ferro-China tonic is a straightforward Game of the Goose, with the favorable throw-doubling spaces in exactly the same sequence as in the parent game. These spaces are marked with a lion's head – the trademark used for the drink. Two lions stare at each other across the *bridge* at space 6, while the *prison* at space 52 becomes a lion's cage. The *well* space at 31 shows the factory dating from 1881 in via Savona, in the heart of Milan - it closed quite recently and has now been turned into housing units. The *death* space at 58 shows an invalid, for whom you must buy a glass of Ferro-China and then start the game again. The red bands marking out the track carry slogans for the tonic. Would you like to be always lively? Drink a Ferro-China before meals. Would you like to have strong sons and daughters? To avoid loss of appetite? To have tranquil sleep? To keep illness away while traveling? Don't forget to take your Ferro-China!

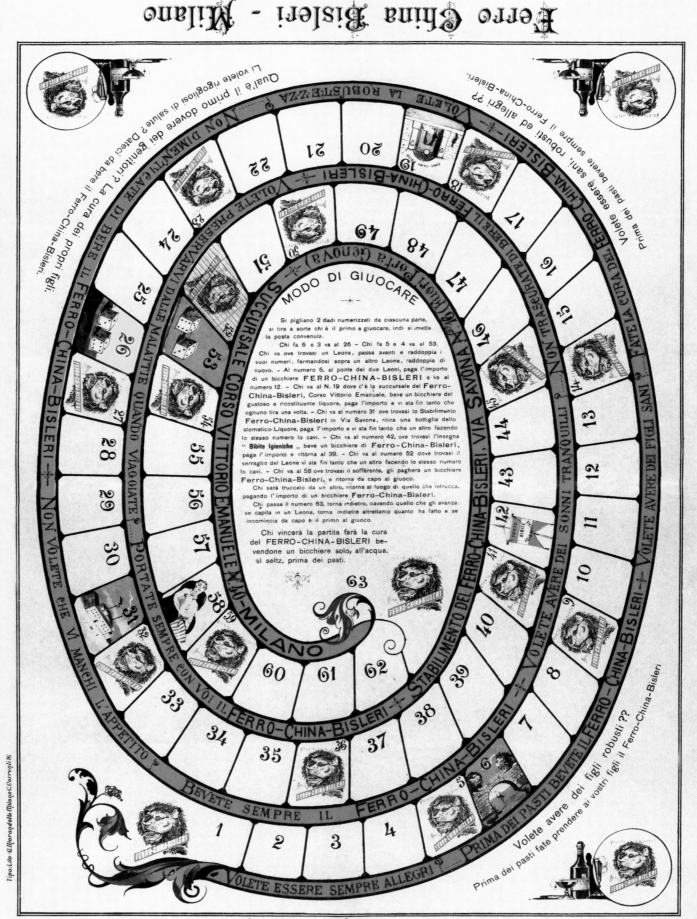

Ferro China Bisleri - Milano

Stabilimento Via Savona N. 16 (fuori P. Genova)

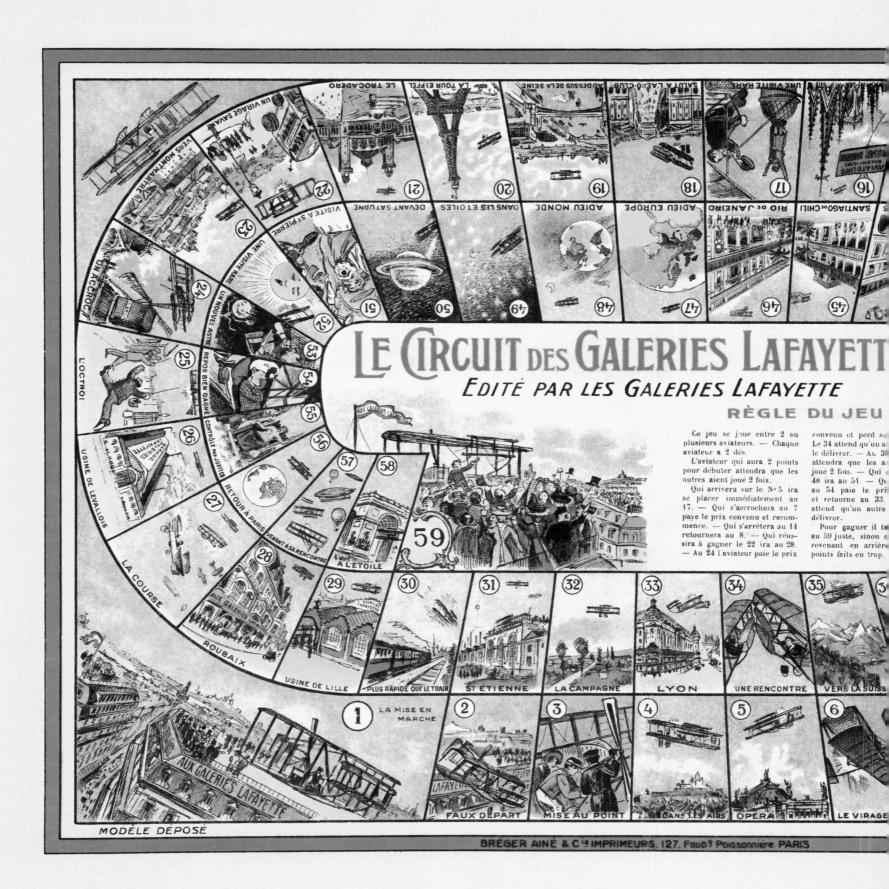

The Circuit of the Galeries Lafayette.
Paris: Galeries Lafayette
about 1906

Aviation was in its infancy when the game of *The Circuit of the Galeries Lafayette* was brought out. After an initial flight in 1903, the Wright Brothers worked on the development of a practical aircraft. The result was the aircraft shown in the game – a Wright Flyer III dating from 1905. Although the aircraft was capable of sustained flights lasting almost an hour, the fantastic feats in the air and in outer space achieved in the game were pure fantasy. However, fantasy would in part be turned to fact when in 1912 the department store issued a challenge, offering a prize of 25,000 francs to anyone who could land a plane safely on its roof – a challenge eventually met only in 1919 when a French airman, Jules Védrines, landed his Caudron G.3 biplane on the rooftop, relying on some judiciously placed sandbags and the strong hands of a few friends to slow the aircraft before it could drop to the streets below. He won the prize outright – but had to pay a small fine for violating air regulations. The game itself is light hearted – there is no *death* space, despite the hazards of early aviation, and a visit to St. Peter on space 51 seems to be going well. Advertising for the *Galeries Lafayette* is confined to showing the international branches of the store, both in Europe and further afield.

Goose Game of Carillon de Flandres chicory. Bourbourg, France Nord: Vilain Frères

about 1910

arillon de Flandres was a brand of chicory made in northern France by the Vilain brothers, sold in packets with a distinctive bell-tower as a logo. Curiously, the game is devoid of targeted product advertising, whether in the illustrations or in the rules, which are completely standard for the Game of the Goose. The throw-doubling spaces marked with a goose are in a single series, spaced by nine, rather than the double series found in the classic game. All the spaces are illustrated in some way. At space 7, is a monoplane, probably a representation of the famous Blériot XI in which the first crossing of the English Channel was made, in 1909. The other non-active spaces illustrate a wide variety of subjects, so that much of the fun of the game for children would have been identifying these. A departure from the usual illustration occurs at space 42, normally showing the *Labyrinth*. Here, though, the space shows a scene of steep mountains – in which it is of course just as easy to lose one's way – with the instruction to return to space 30. Whether children would have been upset by the final image of a goose strung up by the neck, as at the poulterer's shop, is an open question.

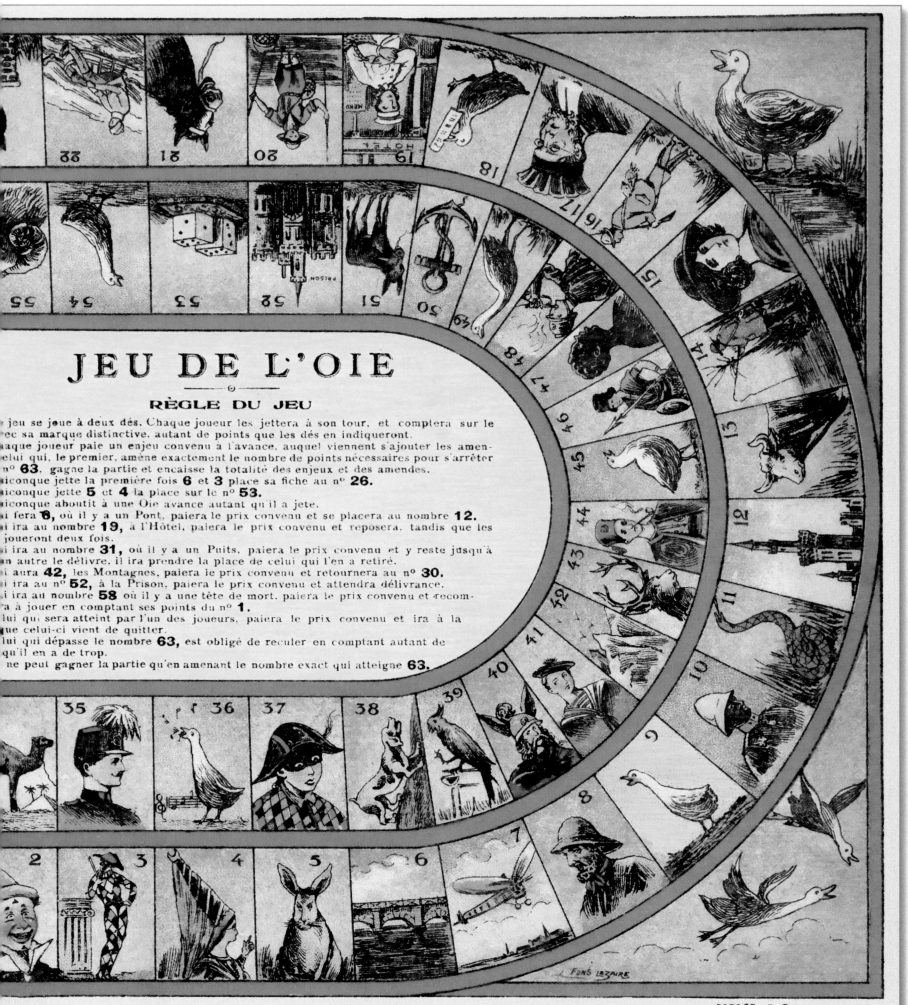

JEU DE L'OIE

RÈGLE DU JEU

...jeu se joue à deux dés. Chaque joueur les jettera à son tour, et comptera sur le ...ec sa marque distinctive, autant de points que les dés en indiqueront.

...aque joueur paie un enjeu convenu à l'avance, auquel viennent s'ajouter les amen-...lui qui, le premier, amène exactement le nombre de points nécessaires pour s'arrêter ...n° **63**, gagne la partie et encaisse la totalité des enjeux et des amendes.

...iconque jette la première fois **6** et **3** place sa fiche au n° **26**.

...iconque jette **5** et **4** la place sur le n° **53**.

...iconque aboutit à une Oie avance autant qu'il a jeté.

...i fera **6**, où il y a un Pont, paiera le prix convenu et se placera au nombre **12**.

...i ira au nombre **19**, à l'Hôtel, paiera le prix convenu et reposera, tandis que les ...joueront deux fois.

...i ira au nombre **31**, où il y a un Puits, paiera le prix convenu et y reste jusqu'à ...un autre le délivre, il ira prendre la place de celui qui l'en a retiré.

...i aura **42**, les Montagnes, paiera le prix convenu et retournera au n° **30**.

...i ira au n° **52**, à la Prison, paiera le prix convenu et attendra délivrance.

...i ira au nombre **58** où il y a une tête de mort, paiera le prix convenu et recom-...ra à jouer en comptant ses points du n° **1**.

...lui qui sera atteint par l'un des joueurs, paiera le prix convenu et ira à la ...que celui-ci vient de quitter.

...lui qui dépasse le nombre **63**, est obligé de reculer en comptant autant de ...qu'il en a de trop.

...ne peut gagner la partie qu'en amenant le nombre exact qui atteigne **63**.

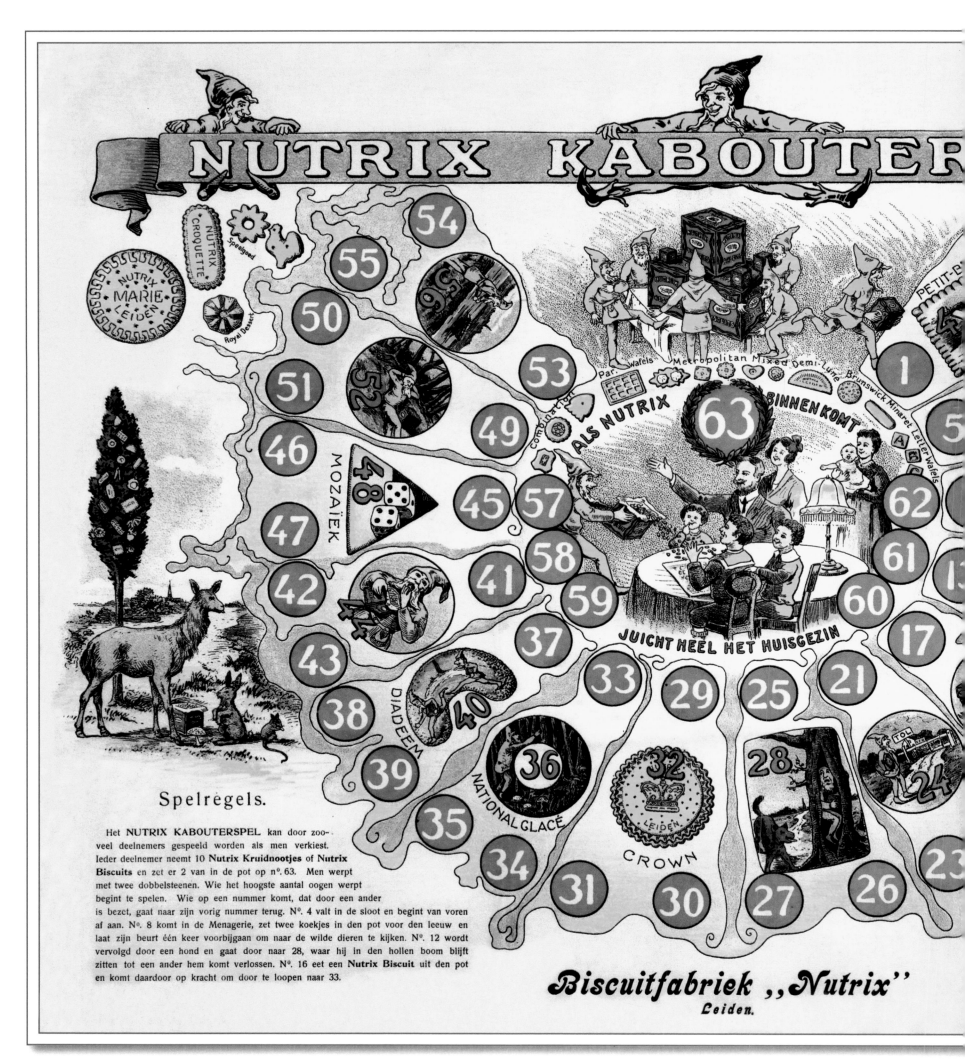

NUTRIX KABOUTER

NUTRIX CROQUETTE

Speelgoed

NUTRIX MARIE LEIDEN

Royal Dessert

54
55
50
56
51
52
53
49
46
48
45
57
MOZAÏEK
47
58
42
41
59
44
43
37
38
DIADEEM
33
29
25
21
39
40
35
36
NATIONAL GLACÉ
32
LEIDEN
CROWN
28
24
34
31
30
27
26
23

63
ALS NUTRIX
BINNEN KOMT
JUICHT HEEL HET HUISGEZIN

PETIT-B
1
5
62
61
13
60
17

Spelregels.

Het NUTRIX KABOUTERSPEL kan door zoo-veel deelnemers gespeeld worden als men verkiest. Ieder deelnemer neemt 10 Nutrix Kruidnootjes of Nutrix Biscuits en zet er 2 van in de pot op n°. 63. Men werpt met twee dobbelsteenen. Wie het hoogste aantal oogen werpt begint te spelen. Wie op een nummer komt, dat door een ander is bezet, gaat naar zijn vorig nummer terug. N°. 4 valt in de sloot en begint van voren af aan. N°. 8 komt in de Menagerie, zet twee koekjes in den pot voor den leeuw en laat zijn beurt één keer voorbijgaan om naar de wilde dieren te kijken. N°. 12 wordt vervolgd door een hond en gaat door naar 28, waar hij in den hollen boom blijft zitten tot een ander hem komt verlossen. N°. 16 eet een Nutrix Biscuit uit den pot en komt daardoor op kracht om door te loopen naar 33.

Biscuitfabriek ,,Nutrix''
Leiden.

SPEL

Boomstam

Klaverblad

Sigaar

Curaçaosche amandel

Frou-Frou

3

6

MENAGERIE

8

7

ALGERIA

12

10

11

16

EIWTBISCUIT

14

15

18

19

Nº. 20 rijdt mee op een boerenwagen en betaalt 2 koekjes voor vracht. Nº. 24 moet een
koekje voor tolgeld geven. Nº. 32 eet een koekje
uit den pot en gaat naar nº. 37. Nº. 36 is ver-
dwaald in het bosch en gaat terug naar nº 10.
Nº. 40 wordt achterhaald en laat tweemaal zijn
beurt voorbijgaan. Nº. 44 eet twee **Nutrix
Biscuits** en begint opnieuw. Nº. 47 betaalt
een biscuit en mag negen punten vooruit. Nº. 52
n slaap gevallen, betaalt twee koekjes voor straf, en laat tweemaal zijn beurt
rbijgaan. Nº. 56 kan niet over het water, betaalt twee koekjes aan den pot
gaat met het bootje naar nº. 57.

Vie nº. 63 bereikt wint het spel en mag alle **Nutrix koekjes** hebben.

Game of Nutrix Dwarves.

Leiden: Nutrix Biscuit Factory

about 1930

Dutch games advertising biscuits were often played with biscuits as stakes. A fine example is this *Game of Nutrix Dwarves*, depicting a fairyland journey, with various imaginative delights and dangers. Each player begins with ten Nutrix biscuits of the kind called *Kruidnoten* (a spicy treat traditionally associated with the early December *Sinterklaas* holiday in the Netherlands) and puts two of these in the pot. Along the way, all the different kinds of biscuits are illustrated and named. At space 8, the Menagerie Lion biscuit is worked into the rules: 'Put two biscuits in the pot for the Lion and stop one turn to see the wild animals.' At various points, the player is directed to eat a biscuit from the pot. But a punishment (at space 44, which shows a gnome busily eating through a large box of biscuits) is to have to eat two of one's own supply — and begin the game again. The central space says: 'If Nutrix comes, the whole family cheers.' Whoever gets there first may have all the Nutrix biscuits.

Board Games Go To America: the Quest for the New

The first printed board games in the USA were imports from London and the earliest American productions in the 1820s were map games based on English models. Even the famous Mansion of Happiness game, often thought of as an American invention, was a close adaptation of a London original.

One of the first games to be advertised in America was the Journey through Europe *invented by John Jeffreys in 1759, already mentioned in Chapter 3. It appeared in a Pennsylvania newspaper of 1775, being included in an advertisement for a remarkably various shipload of goods, ranging from hunting knives and cockspurs to silver shoe buckles. Early in the nineteenth century, advertisements for English games were appearing regularly in all the main centers: New York, Boston, Washington and Pennsylvania. The range available in New York was comparable to that offered in London and stress was laid on 'new' games, especially at Christmas and New Year, when these advertisements mostly appeared. Thus, an advertisement in the* New York Evening Post *of 31st December 1810 offered:*

Juvenile Pastimes, played with Totum and Counters viz.

Game of the Jew, Pastora, Magic Ring, Bulwark of Britannia, Reward of Merit, Game of Human Life, Elegant Amusements, Geographical Games of Europe, England and the world.

These advertisements do not mention the Game of the Goose, presumably because it was considered old-fashioned and too dull for the American market.

The earliest games produced in America were in fact geographical games, clearly derived from map-based English models. Two publishers brought out very similar games in 1822. F and R Lockwood of New York brought out the Travelers' Tour of the United States, *reproduced in this chapter. The other contender for the earliest American game is Edward Parker's* The Geographical Pastime or Complete Tour of Europe, *surviving in only one example. It is not dated with a calendar date, so the precedence is uncertain.*

In the period from 1830 to about 1860, hundreds of thousands of British people emigrated to the United States, working in agriculture, in mining and in the large industrial centers of New England and the Mid-Atlantic coast. At least one British manufacturer thought it worthwhile to provide a game to introduce them to their new home. That game was The Star-Spangled Banner, or Emigrants to the United States. *Its beautifully detailed scenes – confined to the Eastern half of the country - give a vivid account of the USA before the Californian gold-rush of the 1850s.*

The first game produced in America to have a significant market impact was The Mansion of Happiness – an instructive, moral and amusing entertainment. *The first American edition was published in 1843 by W. & S. B. Ives, in Salem, Mass. and was reissued several times by Ives and subsequently by Parker Brothers in 1894, when they included on the game board the claim, 'The first board game ever published in America'. Though the claim proved to be unjustified, the game remains an important landmark in the history of U.S. printed board games. By contrast, the* Game of the Goose *had little impact, even though it did appear in a few American editions around 1850.*

A very different reflection of the close cultural links between Western Europe and the United States was the appearance of a novel by Jules Verne, The Testament of an Eccentric. *In the story, the rival heirs to the fortune of a very eccentric Chicago millionaire fight it out by being part of a gigantic Goose game played across America, enabling Verne to write a novel of travel and excitement on a unique (and truly incredible) plan.*

A more famous novel by Jules Verne, Around the World in Eighty Days, *indirectly inspired another board game,* Nellie Bly. *The game tells the story of her round-the world journey, in which she succeeded in beating the fictional target of the novel. And another famous European novel,* Robinson Crusoe, *inspired a colorful lithographed game by Milton Bradley towards the end of the nineteenth century.*

Typical of the American spirit was the game of the Errand Boy, *showing the possibilities open to even those of humble station in life. The game emphasized the qualities needed to succeed within the American Dream: honesty, hard work and intelligence. But success here meant making enough money to become an 'Honorable and Respected Banker & a Good Citizen' – perhaps not so straightforward an objective in our questioning times. For the* Shop Boy, *a humbler game of the same period, 'success' simply meant getting behind the counter, rather than sweeping the floor of the shop.*

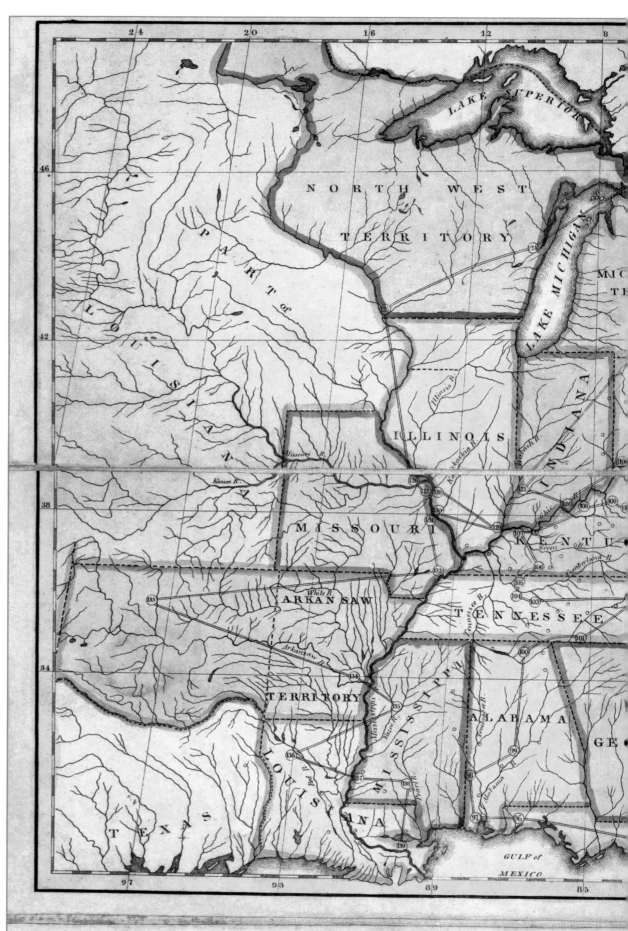

The Travelers' Tour through

the United States.

New York: Lockwood

1822

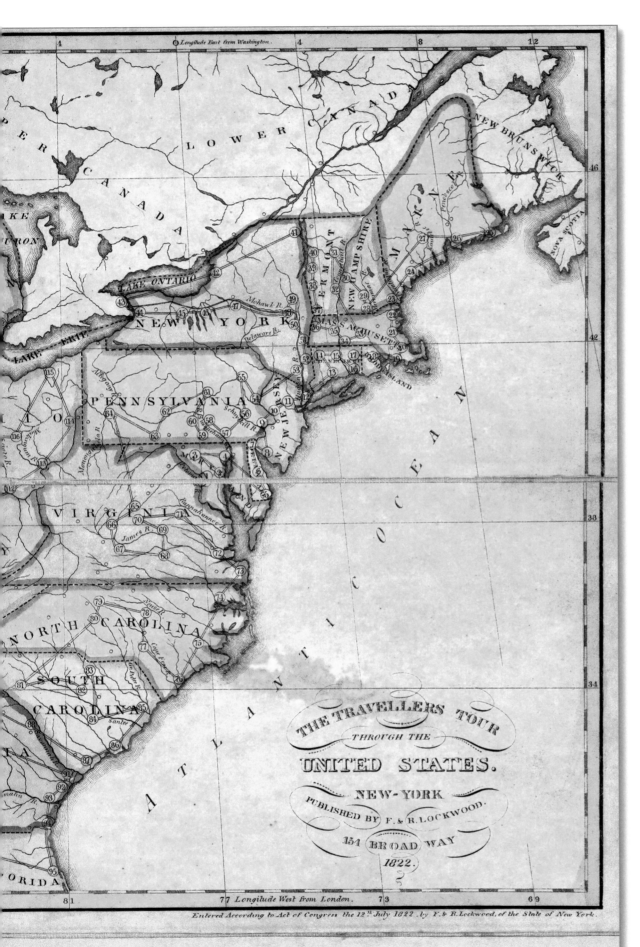

The *Travelers' Tour through the United States* consists of a map of the Eastern states, going only as far west as the boundary of Arkensaw Territory. The track, consisting of numbered circles, begins at Washington City and ends at New Orleans (the winning space, number 139). The rules list the places corresponding to the circles, with a brief description and – for towns – the size of their population. The places are not named on the map and here lies the interest of the game. Players had to name the places they landed on *without* referring to the rules. To make the game more difficult, the players might agree to give the population of each place, or lose their turn. The descriptions of the places are mainly informative, for example: 'New York is the first commercial city in America. The revenue from the customs collected at this port is about one fourth of the whole revenue of the United States'. But some of the descriptions are endearing: 'The citizens of Charleston (space 86) are distinguished for polished manners and unaffected hospitality'.

Game of the Star-Spangled Banner, or Emigrants

to the United States. London: Wallis

1830

This beautiful game of 147 spaces begins with the Great Sea Serpent 'rearing its head as high as the topmast of a ship' and ends at New York City. The game is played by drawing numbered cards from a bag, which, the rule booklet says, 'is more lively' than using dice or a teetotum. The State Capitals give an extra turn: 'Observe that as each State has its own independent government and cannot be controlled from Washington ... whoever arrives at one of these spaces has the privilege of drawing again immediately'. Several spaces have vivid special instructions, for example:

Space 10: *Turkey Buzzard* — This bird feeds on carrion and if attempted to be taken vomits the contents of its stomach into the face of its pursuer ... *Get out of its way and begin again.*

Space 20: *Settler's Hut* — Built with logs and surrounded with a fence of stakes. *Stop one drawing to try how you like it.*

Space 44: *WASHINGTON* — The seat of general government ... The city is planned on a most magnificent scale but at present consists principally of a few inferior houses, with the Post-Office, Bank and a splendid Capitol or House of Representatives... *Go on to No. 73.*

Space 90: *Lynch Law* (Arkansas) — An odious practice, too frequently indulged in, in the states which are at a great distance from the general government. It is no other than a mockery of justice ... *Go back to No. 67 (Woodcutter's hut).*

This game gives a fine sense of how much America has changed in two centuries.

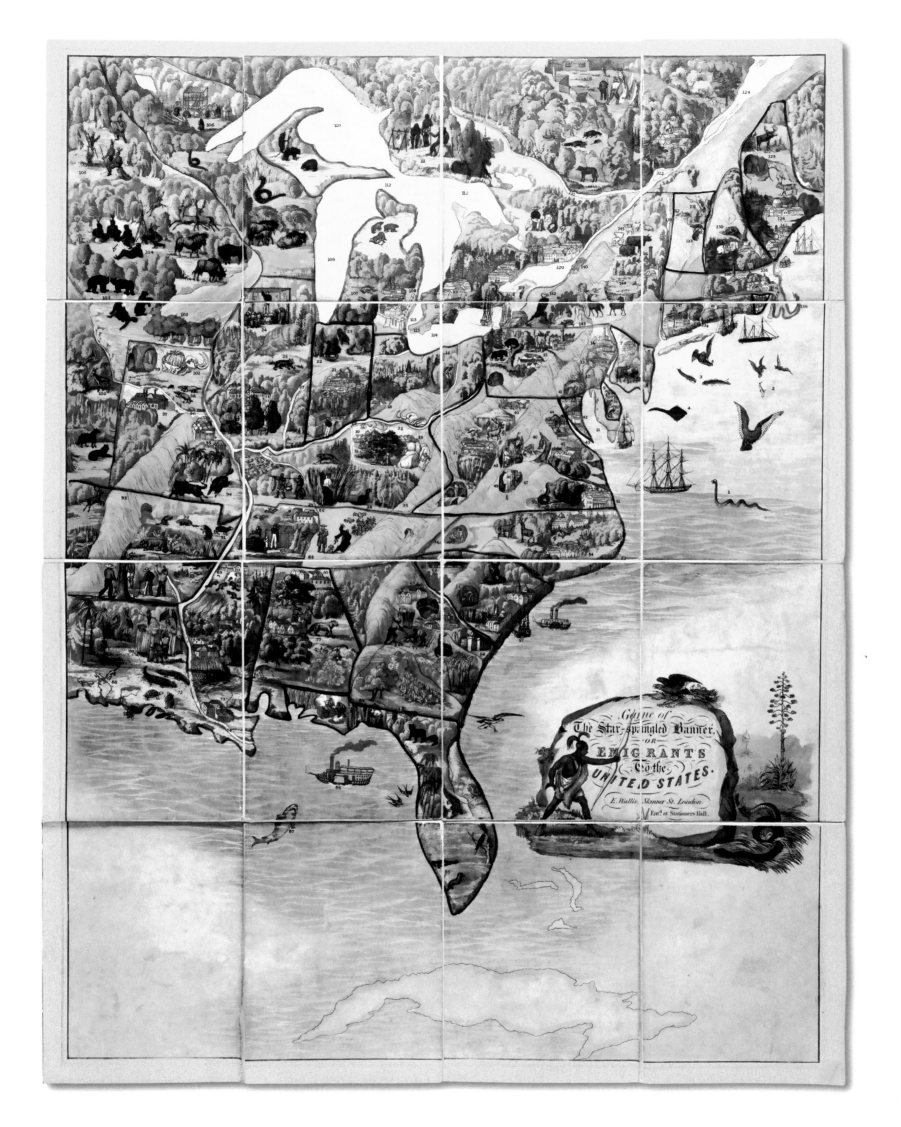

Game of
The Star-spangled Banner,
OR
EMIGRANTS
To the
UNITED STATES.

E. Wallis, Skinner St. London.

Emd at Stationers Hall.

The Mansion of Happiness. First published Salem MA

1843, this edition Salem & Boston: Ives, 1864

*T*he *Mansion of Happiness* game was first published in London in 1800 by Robert Laurie and James Whittle. Although there were no throw-doubling spaces, there was a series of spaces that advance the player by six towards the winning space, showing the Mansion of Happiness: these represented virtues such as Piety, Honesty, Sobriety and Gratitude. On the other hand, the rules provided that anyone landing on the vices of Audacity, Cruelty, Immodesty, or Ingratitude 'must return to his former situation and not even *think* of happiness, much less partake of it.' All these features were retained in the American editions, such as that illustrated here, though some changes were made. English references to the London prisons of Bridewell and Newgate were replaced by the House of Correction (space 30) and the Prison (space 50). There is no penalty for landing on either of these spaces, but players may be sent there for specific crimes, e.g. the *robber* [anyone landing on space 57] must be sent to prison for two months [i.e. lose two turns] but may be released if another player is sent there. A significant difference is that the American game was not played for stakes. No doubt it was felt that a gambling element was inappropriate for a game with a claim to high moral values.

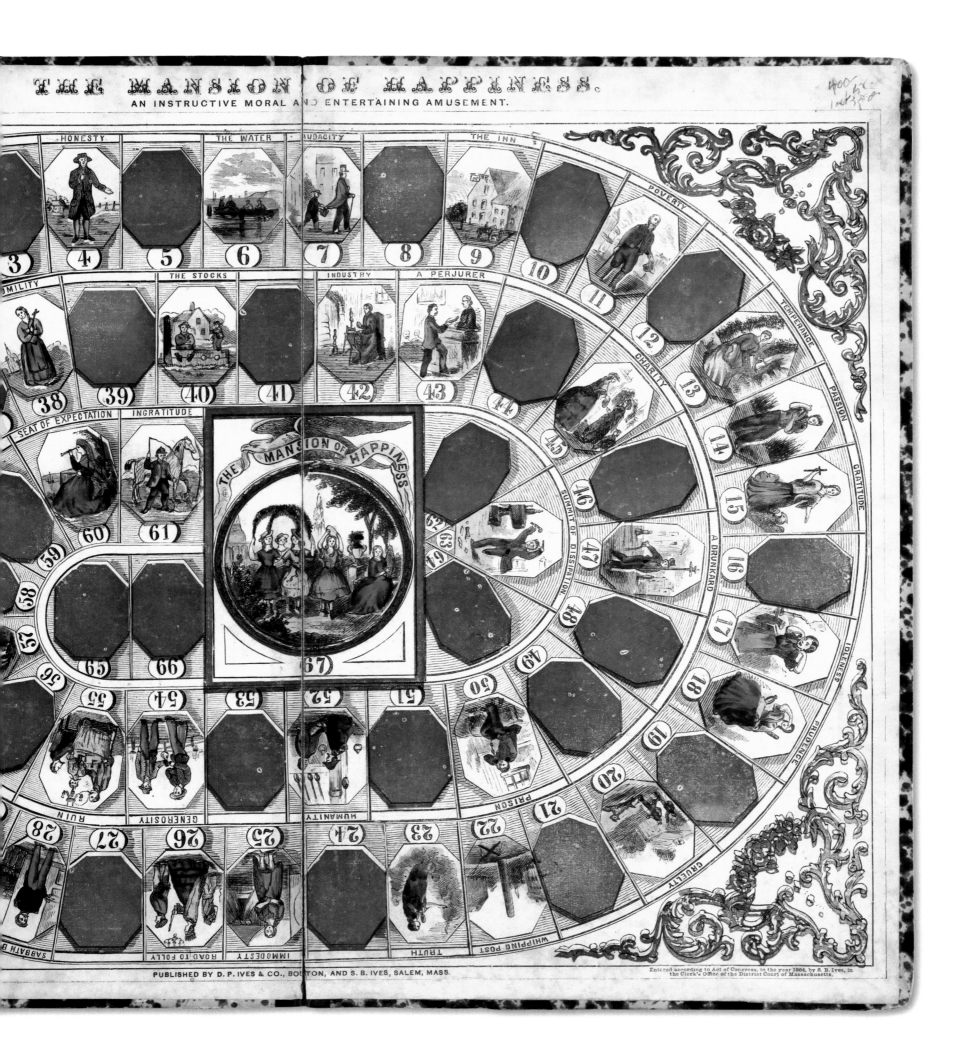

THE MANSION OF HAPPINESS.

AN INSTRUCTIVE MORAL AND ENTERTAINING AMUSEMENT.

PUBLISHED BY D. P. IVES & CO., BOSTON, AND S. B. IVES, SALEM, MASS.

Entered according to Act of Congress, in the year 1864, by S. B. Ives, in the Clerk's Office of the District Court of Massachusetts.

*Game of Goose. Designed by Mary
D. Carroll. Providence RI:
Knowles, Anthony*

1855

Examples of the classic *Game of the Goose* in the USA are very rare. The example shown, copyrighted by Mary D. Carroll in Rhode Island in 1855, is not quite the earliest Goose game to be published in America. In 1851, J. P. Beach of New York City had published the *Jolly Game of Goose* to a design in the shape of a goose copied (in reverse) from an English original. Although Mary Carroll's game is in most respects a classic Game of the Goose, the geese usually on spaces 5 and 9 are absent. This is a feature of several English goose games, including that shown in Chapter 1, and suggests that she used an English game as her source. However, her charming rural decoration of the end space, with bees buzzing happily round the hive, is surely a representation of the American settler's dream.

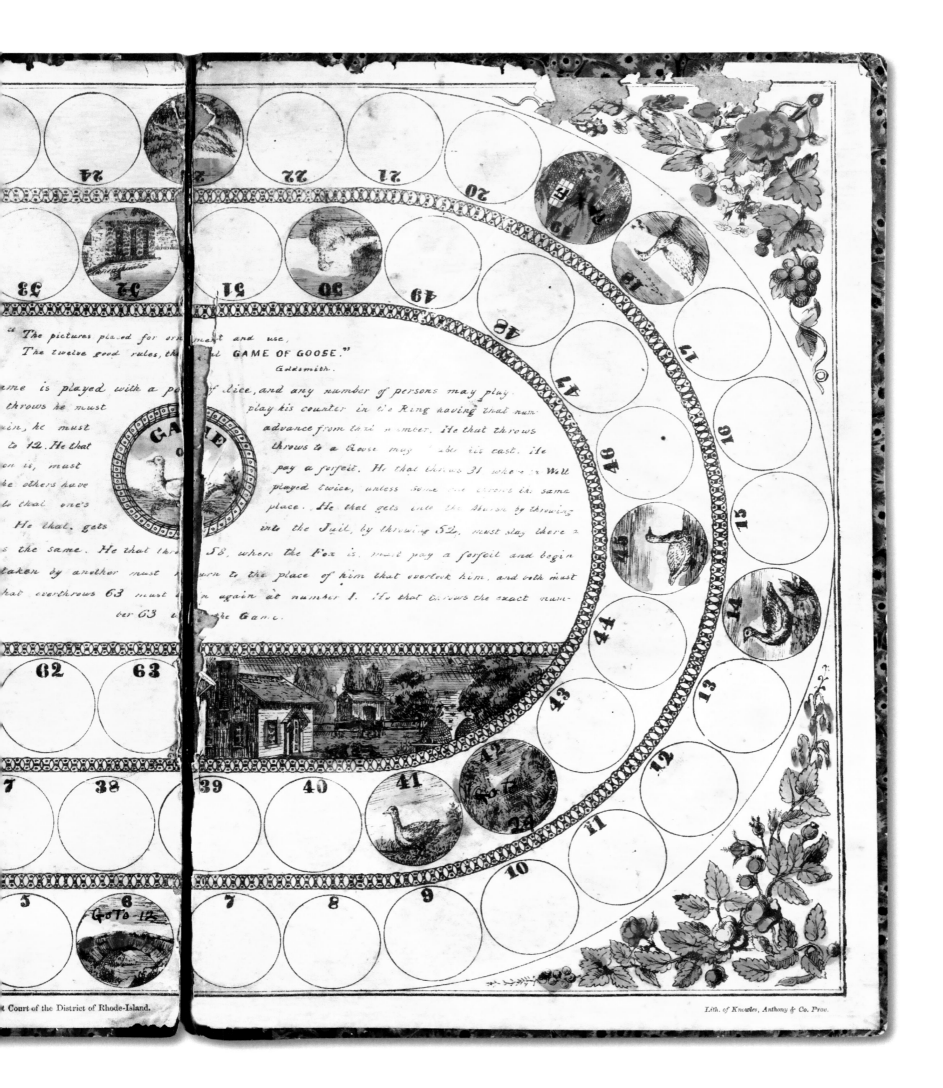

"The pictures placed for ornament and use,
The twelve good rules, the ____ GAME OF GOOSE."

Goldsmith.

____ame is played with a pa____ of dice, and any number of persons may play. ____ throws he must ____ play his counter in the Ring having that num____ ____in, he must ____ advance from that number. He that throws ____ to 12. He that ____ throws to a Goose may ____ the his cast. He ____ ____on is, must ____ pay a forfeit. He that throws 31 where the Well ____ ____he others have ____ played twice, unless some one throws in the same ____ ____to that one's ____ place. He that gets into the Shrew by throwing ____ He that gets ____ into the Jail, by throwing 52, must stay there a ____ ____s the same. He that thr____ 58, where the Fox is, must pay a forfeit and begin ____ ____taken by another must return to the place of him that overtook him, and both must ____ ____hat overthrows 63 must ____n again at number 1. He that throws the exact num____ ber 63 w____ the Game.

GAME o____

62   63

7   38   39   40   41   42   Go t____   24

5   6   7   8   9   10   11

Go To 12

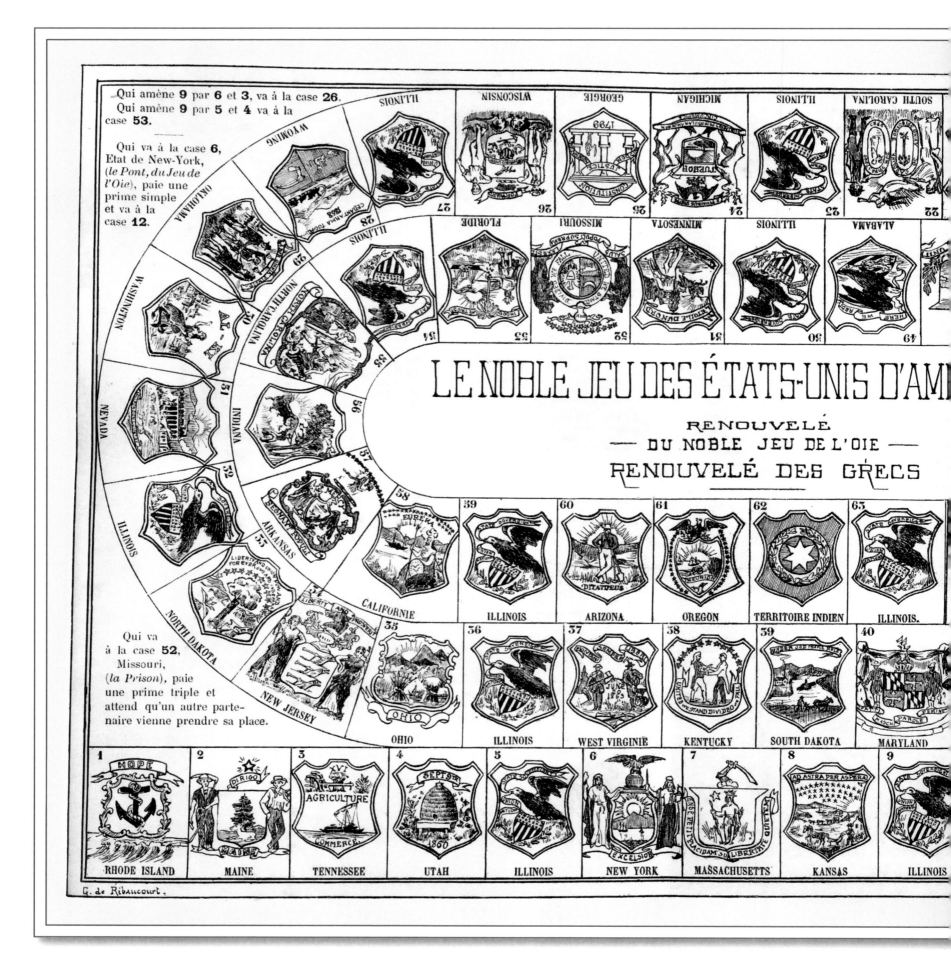

Qui va à la case **19**, Louisiane, (*l'Hôtellerie*), paye une prime double et reste deux coups sans jouer.

Qui va à la case **31**, Nevada, (*le Puits*), paie une prime triple et reste jusqu'à ce qu'un autre joueur le délivre

Qui va à la case **42**, Nebraska, (*le La-byrinthe*), paie une prime simple et va à la case **30**.

...LE DU JEU

...e est gagnée par celui
...le premier la case **63**.

...*Illinois* remplace l'Oie,
...s ne peuvent s'y arrêter,
...t redoubler les points

...n joueur est rencon-
...autre, il paie une
...ple et doit revenir
...précédemment
...r celui-ci.

Qui va à la case **58**, Californie, (*la Mort*), paie une prime triple et retourne à la case **1** pour recommencer la partie au coup suivant.

The Noble Game of the United States of America. Designed by Jules Verne. Paris: Hetzel

1899

Jules Verne's novel, *The Testament of an Eccentric*, tells the story of a millionaire, William J. Hypperbone, whose will provides that his fortune of 60 million US dollars should go to the winner of a fantastic game of Goose. The contestants must travel through the states and territories of America according to the throw of dice at the office of Hypperbone's attorney. Their adventures — incorporating much travelog detail — are the basis of the novel. Included is a fold-out game of the United States, shown here, in which the various states and territories are shown by their official seals. The correspondences to the classic Goose game are cleverly done. All the *goose* spaces show Illinois, whose state seal incorporates the American eagle. New York is an obvious choice for the *bridge*, at 6. The *prison* space at 52 shows Missouri, home of the notorious Missouri State Penitentiary in Jefferson City, the largest prison in the world at the time. The *death* space at 58 shows California: a trip to Death Valley is in prospect. Finally, the winning space at 63 again shows Illinois: the attorney's office, where the game ends, is supposed to be in Chicago.

Nellie Bly. New York: Singer

about 1898

In contrast to the fictional travelers in the previous game, Nellie Bly was entirely real, even if that was just her pen name. She was in fact Elizabeth Cochrane Seaman, an American journalist born in 1864, and it was she who persuaded her editor at the *New York World* to let her emulate and improve upon the travels of Phileas Fogg in *Around the World in Eighty Days*. The game shows her progress day-by-day, beginning in Hoboken, NJ, on November 14, 1889, when she set sail for Southampton, England in the ocean liner *Augusta Victoria*. On the ninth day, she was in Amiens, meeting Jules Verne himself. Her journey took her through the Suez Canal (day 13) and on to Hong Kong and Japan. For the final ocean leg, she sailed on the *Oceanic*, but the ship was delayed by storms and arrived at San Francisco two days behind schedule. However, the owner of the *New York World*, Joseph Pulitzer, chartered a private train to bring her back to New York at high speed, and it is this train that is featured in the final central decoration of the game. The train averaged a record-breaking 37 miles per hour in its coast-to-coast journey, taking priority over other rail traffic, though it stopped at small towns for publicity opportunities. The final time for the round trip, just over 72 days, stood as a record for only a few months.

Robinson Crusoe. Springfield MA: Milton Bradley

about 1900

CALM.

STIFF BREEZE

BREAKERS.

M. BRADLEY & Co. LITH. SPRINGFIELD, MASS.

Milton Bradley was a key figure in the development of American games. A draughtsman and lithographer, he published *The Checkered Game of Life* in 1860 as a sideline to his lithography business. This was a 'morality' game and, thanks to Bradley's improvements in lithographic printing, could be mass produced at an economic cost. In 1870, he brought out a game of *Robinson Crusoe*, based on the novel by Daniel Defoe. The later version shown here is marked on the reverse of the board as an 'improved' edition. It is an example of a parallel track game: each of the four tracks is followed separately by an individual player, starting from one of the four corner spaces. The hazard spaces are marked with a black star and labeled as *storm, calm, breakers,* or *stiff breeze*. To make the game fair as between the players, each track is of the same length and encounters the same number of hazards, though these are not in the same order for each track. One of the attractions of this simple dice game is the artistic lithography, with its splendid decorative border in full color.

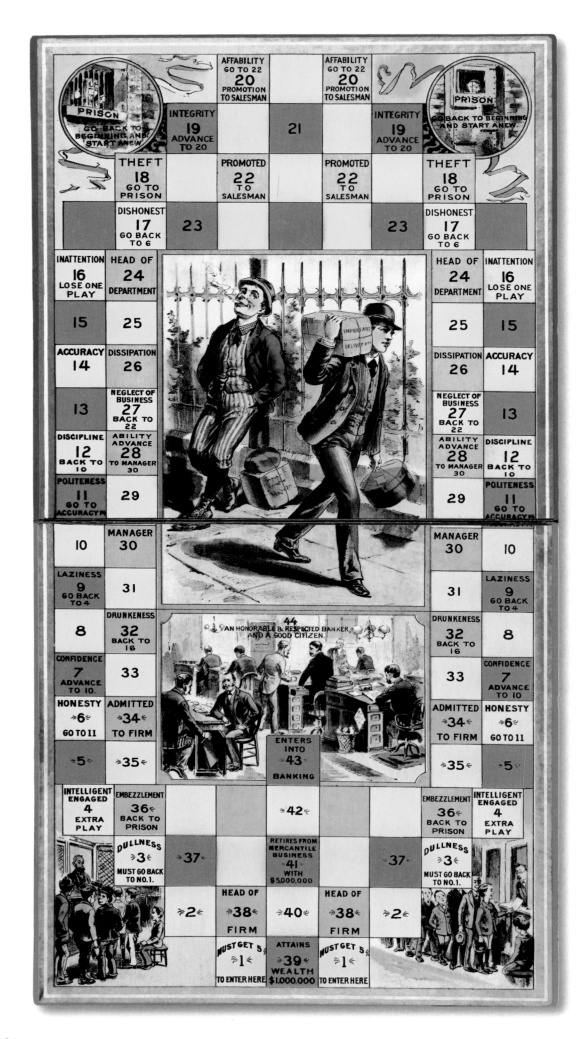

Errand Boy. New York:
McLoughlin Brothers

1891

McLoughlin Brothers, formed in 1858, is perhaps the fountainhead of American game companies. The company produced some of the most beautiful games ever published in the United States, reaching a peak in the 1880s and 1890s before being bought out by Milton Bradley in 1920. The example of their games shown here charts the progress of the humble Errand Boy to becoming a Banker at space 43 and winning the game. The initial part of the track is doubled, so that the player may start on either side of the board. There are several stages in the progress, as the Boy successively becomes a Salesman (space 22), Head of Department (space 24), Manager (space 30), Admitted to Firm (space 34), and Head of Firm (space 38), before attaining wealth of $1,000,000 (space 39). Retiring from mercantile business with $5,000,000 (space 41) is the ultimate achievement and enough to become a Banker at the winning space 44. The progress can be hastened by landing on spaces such as Honesty, Politeness and Accuracy, whereas faults such as Laziness or Inattention will set you back or slow you down. The main hazard is being sent to prison for Theft (space 18) or Embezzlement (space 36); it is necessary to spin 5 to get out of prison and even then you must start again.

204

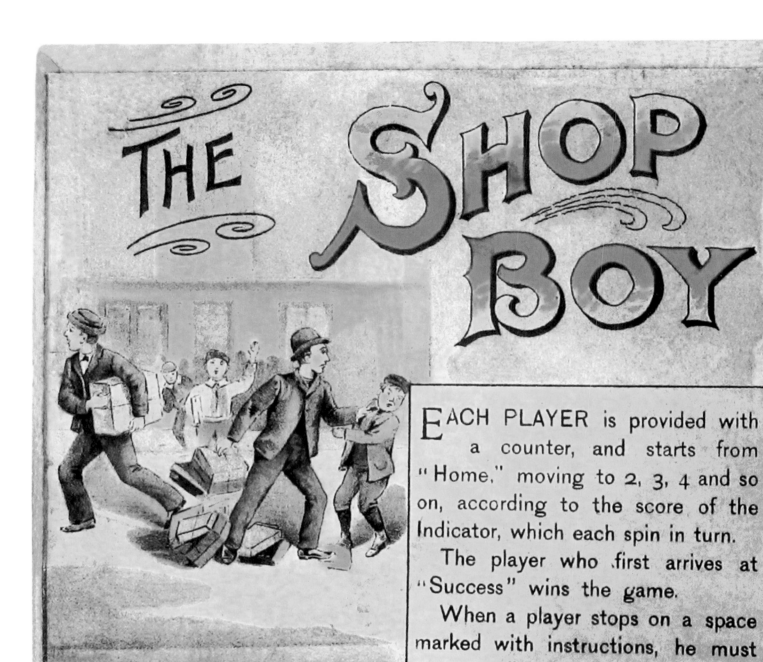

EACH PLAYER is provided with a counter, and starts from "Home," moving to 2, 3, 4 and so on, according to the score of the Indicator, which each spin in turn.

The player who first arrives at "Success" wins the game.

When a player stops on a space marked with instructions, he must act accordingly.

MANUFACTURED BY

J. H. SINGER, NEW YORK.

Shop Boy. New York: Singer

1890s

15 | 14 | 13 | 12 | 11 | 10 EARLY GO TO 18 | 9 | 8

16 LATE GO HOME | 39 | 38 | 37 | 36 | 35 | 34 HONESTY GO TO 41 | 7

17 | 40 PROMPT GO TO CASHIER | 51 | | CASHIER 50 | 33 | 6

18 | 41 | | | 32 | 5

19 | 42 | | | 31 | 4 START AGAIN

20 | 43 TEMPER GO TO CHURCH | 52 LOSE NEXT TURN | 53 SUCCESS | 49 | SALESMAN 30 | 3

21 | 44 | 45 | 46 | 47 TIRED GO TO BED | 48 | 29 SLOW GO TO 17 | 2

22 | 23 GOOD BOY GO TO SALESMAN | 24 | 25 | 26 | 27 | 28 | HOME 1

This simple example shows how board games were presented in the United States at the lower end of the market. The colorful game sheet was glued to the bottom of a box, whose lid would also have a bright and attractive scene, to tempt the purchaser. Indeed, for some US collectors, the box lid is the most sought-after element, rather than the game itself. This box lid shows boys of various ages delivering parcels from the shop - no doubt the first employment for many youngsters, with the ever-present fear of dropping the goods in the street, as the illustration depicts. The game came with a spinner, rather than dice, though the example shown has sadly lost its spinning arrow. The maximum spin of four would make for a rather slow game, as compared with the double-dice excitement of the Goose game. This game would have been understood immediately by young employees: 'late – go home' must have been a familiar reprimand, though 'tired – go to bed' was perhaps not the most usual response of an employer to yawning on the job, however inviting the bed shown at space 19 might appear.

Biography

Adrian Seville is an international expert on the cultural history of printed board games and has lectured widely on his research, both in Europe and America. He studied at Cambridge and Edinburgh universities before joining the staff of City University, London, where he was Academic Registrar. His New York exhibition of board games at the Grolier Club in 2016 was described by the Wall Street Journal as 'a mind-opening cultural event'.

Photo credits

Editorial project VALERIA MANFERTO DE FABIANIS
Editorial coordination GIORGIA RAINERI
Graphic design MARIA CUCCHI

WHITE STAR PUBLISHERS

WS White Star Publishers® is a registered trademark
property of White Star s.r.l.

© 2019 White Star s.r.l.
Piazzale Luigi Cadorna, 6 - 20123 Milan, Italy
www.whitestar.it

Editing: Inga Sempel

ISBN 978-88-544-1519-5
1 2 3 4 5 6   23 22 21 20 19

Printed in Italy by Rotolito S.p.A. - Seggiano di Pioltello (Milan)

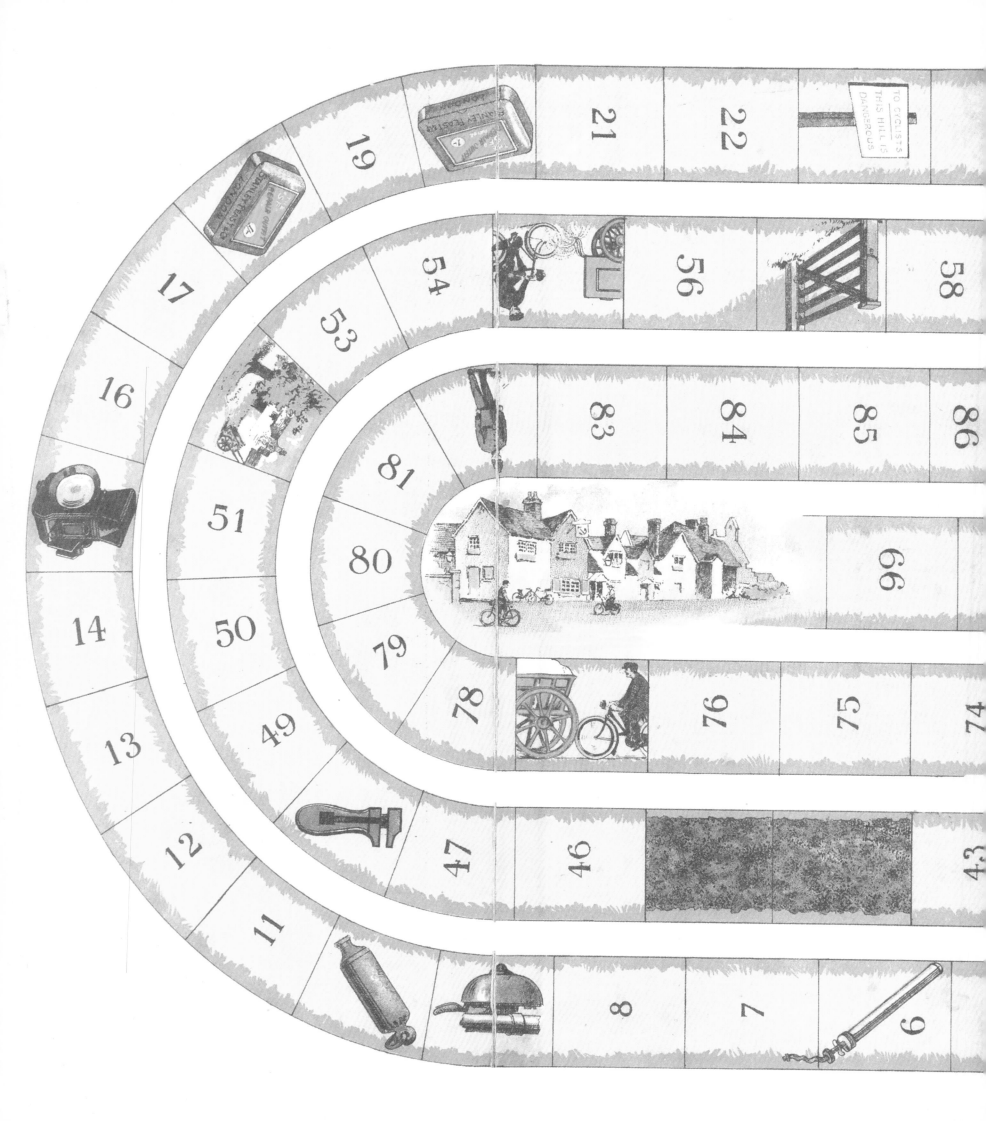